BIG ENGLISH ② PLUS

Contents

In My Classroom

1 🎧 **Listen and number.**

2 **Look at 1. Circle.**

1 They're **colouring** / **counting**.

2 She's **writing** / **playing** a game.

3 They're **using the computer** / **listening**.

4 She's **gluing** / **counting**.

5 He's **writing** / **using the computer**.

6 He's **cutting** / **watching a DVD**.

3 Listen and sing. Then match and write.

a

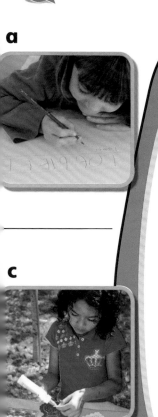

_____

b

_____

c

_____

d

_____

Here's My Classroom!

Look! Here's my classroom.
And here are my friends!
Peter, Sarah and Timothy,
Penny, Jack and Jen!

Peter is cutting paper.
Penny is writing her name.
Sarah is listening to a story.
And Jack is playing a game.

Timothy is counting.
Jen is gluing.
We have fun and learn a lot.
What are your friends doing?

4 Draw your classroom. Then say.

5 **Read and write.**

1 How many Marias are there in the class?

There are _____ Marias.

2 What is one Maria doing?

She's _____ and

_____.

3 What is the other Maria doing?

She's _____.

THINK BIG

What do you like doing? Read and circle.

using the computer   writing   reading

listening   cutting   gluing

watching a DVD   playing a game

6 **Look and match. Then say.**

1 What's she doing?

She's listening to a story.

a

2 What are they doing?

They're watching a DVD.

b

3 What's he doing?

He's gluing shapes.

c

7 **Listen. Follow the path.**

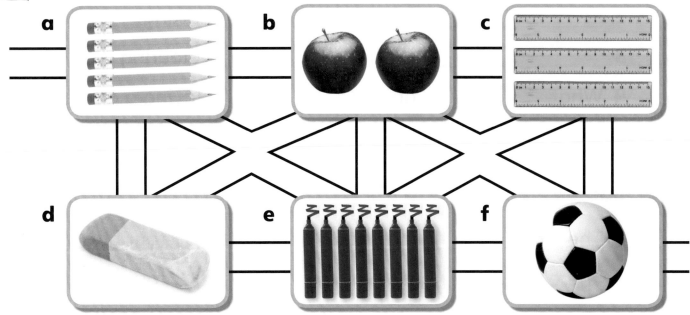

8 **Look and write.**

| are they (x2) | He's (x2) | She's | They're (x2) | What's he (x2) | What's she |

1 What _____ doing? _____ listening.

2 _____ doing? _____ cutting.

3 _____ doing? _____ colouring.

4 What _____ doing? _____ playing a game.

5 _____ doing? _____ counting.

9 **Look at 8. Read and ✓.**

1 There are ☐ one ball. ☐ four backpacks.

2 There's ☐ one ball. ☐ four backpacks.

10 **Write the words and the number.**

equals (x2)   minus   plus

1

6 pencils _____   +   6 pencils _____ = ☐ pencils.

2

10 footballs _____   –   5 footballs _____ = ☐ footballs.

11 **Listen and read. Write +, –, = and the number.**

1

14 apples   minus   8 apples   equals   ☐ apples.

2

10 marker pens   plus   2 marker pens   equals   ☐ marker pens.

3

6 shapes   plus   8 shapes   equals   ☐ shapes.

12 **Look at 11. Match and write 1–3.**

☐ **a** Six plus eight equals fourteen.
☐ **b** Fourteen minus eight equals six.
☐ **c** Ten plus two equals twelve.

13 **Write the sums using numbers, +, – and =. Then do the sums.**

1 sixty plus seven equals ?

_____

2 eighty-six minus three equals ?

_____

3 twenty-three plus thirty-one equals ?

_____

4 seventy-four minus twelve equals ?

_____

5 sixty plus ten equals ?

_____

6 thirty minus nineteen equals ?

_____

THINK BIG **Write. What two things do you count every day in your classroom?**

_____ and _____

14 Read and match.

a

1 Write.
2 Don't play a game.
3 Don't use the computer.
4 Count.

b

c

d

15 Read and circle.

1 **Stand** / **Sit** down.   2 Don't **stand** / **sit** up!
3 **Write** / **Close** your books.   4 Don't **colour** / **write** the picture.
5 **Open** / **Write** your name.   6 Don't **cut** / **write** the paper.

16 Look and write.

cut ✗   eat ✗   listen ✓   write ✓

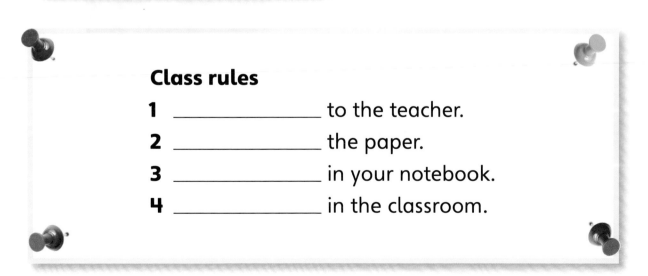

Class rules

1 _____ to the teacher.
2 _____ the paper.
3 _____ in your notebook.
4 _____ in the classroom.

17 **Look at the pictures in 18 . Read and write.**

> cold   flowers   open   trees

1 It's _____ in the mountains.

2 There are tall _____ in the forest.

3 The school on the boat isn't closed. It's _____.

4 There are colourful _____ in the garden.

18 **Listen, read and match. Write a–d.**

1 They're studying in a classroom on ☐

2 They're growing plants and flowers in ☐

3 They're having a P.E. class in ☐

4 They're studying animals in ☐

a a forest in Turkey. There are lots of animals and birds in the trees.

b a boat in Bangladesh. This school is always open.

c a garden in the United States. It's a Science class.

d the snow in France. The school is in the mountains.

19 **Look at 18. Read and write.**

| Bangladesh   France   the United States   Turkey |

1 The pupils in _____ are in the forest.
2 There is a garden at the school in _____.
3 The boat school is in _____.
4 The pupils in _____ are in the mountains.

20 **Find and write the sentences. Then match.**

1 country. wet It a is

_____

a France

2 trees are There the in forest.

_____

b the United States

3 children skiing. The love

_____

c Turkey

4 garden are There flowers the in

_____

d Bangladesh

Circle and draw.

THINK BIG My favourite classroom is **in the mountains / in a forest / on a boat / in a garden**.

21 **Read and match. Then say.**

a

1 May I use the marker pens now?

b

2 Yes, let's take turns!

c

3 It's fun taking turns!

22 **Read and write.**

fun Let's May now

Anita: _____ I use the computer _____?
Sam: Yes! _____ take turns.
Anita: OK. It's _____ taking turns!

23 **Find and circle the letters th.**

24 **Read and circle the letters th.**

1 bath   **2** path   **3** this   **4** that

25 **Match the words with the same sounds.**

1 they   **a** thin
2 Maths   **b** then

26 **Listen and chant.**

There are three
Crocodiles in the bath.
They've got thin mouths
But big teeth!
Look out! Look out!

27 **Look and write.**

counting   cutting   playing a game   using the computer

1 What's she doing?
She's _____.

2 What's he doing?
He's _____.

3 What are they doing?
They're _____.

4 What are they doing?
They're _____.

28 **Count and write the numbers. Circle There's or There are.**

Our Classroom	
computer	I
chairs	IIIII IIIII IIIII III
rubbers	IIIII III
desks	IIIII IIII
teacher	I

1 **There's / There are** ____ computer.

2 **There's / There are** ____ chairs.

3 **There's / There are** ____ rubbers.

4 **There's / There are** ____ desks.

5 **There's / There are** ____ teacher.

29 **Find the words. Circle.**

colouring   counting   cutting   gluing   listening   writing

e	s	g	l	u	i	n	g	m	c
m	i	n	g	i	l	u	r	e	o
n	g	a	t	f	a	s	g	k	u
g	o	t	a	l	k	i	n	g	n
c	o	l	o	u	r	i	n	g	t
u	n	g	t	u	n	g	l	d	i
t	g	o	i	f	g	a	u	g	n
t	l	i	s	t	e	n	i	n	g
i	s	w	r	i	t	i	n	g	a
n	p	a	e	n	t	t	g	i	t
g	i	f	o	i	a	s	f	n	o

30 **Circle and write.**

1 11 marker pens **+ / −** ☐ marker pens = 7 marker pens

2 18 pencils **+ / −** ☐ pencils = 20 pencils

3 13 books **+ / −** ☐ books = 1 book

31 **Complete the table.**

Write your name.	1 _____
Listen.	2 _____
3 _____	Don't open your book.
Sit here.	4 _____
5 _____	Don't use a pencil.

My Games

1 **Read and match. Then say.**

a

1 doing gymnastics

2 flying kites

b

c

3 ice skating

d

4 skateboarding

e

5 playing tennis

f

6 climbing trees

2 Listen and sing. Then match.

Come On and Play

We're playing in the playground.
There are a lot of games to play.
Football, tennis and volleyball.
What do you want to play today?

Paul likes playing on the swings.
Emma likes running and climbing.
We all love riding our bikes.
Tell us! What do you like doing?

We're playing in the playground.
It's always so much fun.
Come on and play with us.
We play with everyone!

a
b
c
d

3 Draw. Then say.

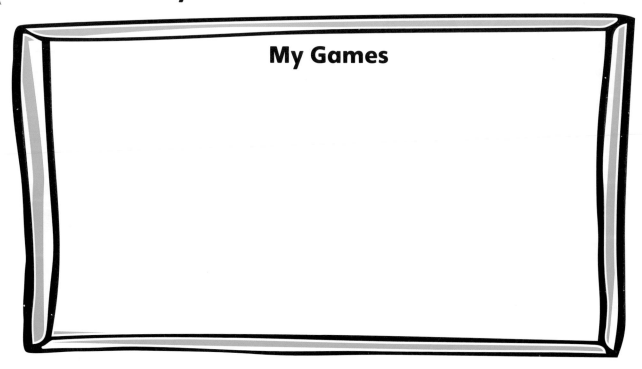

My Games

4 Read and write.

We Like Playing Together!

I like playing football. My sister loves skateboarding.

What does your brother like doing?

He loves playing volleyball.

We like playing together, too.

How can you do that?

1 What does Jamie like doing?

He likes _____.

2 What does Jenny love doing?

She loves _____.

3 What does Tony love doing?

He loves _____.

4 What do they all like doing?

They like _____.

 Circle the odd one out.

5 **Write do or does. Then listen and match.**

1 What _____ he love doing?

a

2 What _____ they like doing?

b

3 What _____ she like doing?

c

4 What _____ they love doing?

d

6 **Look at 5. Write the answers.**

1 He loves _____.

2 They like _____.

3 She likes _____.

4 They love _____.

7 **Read and ✓.**

1 I like skateboarding.

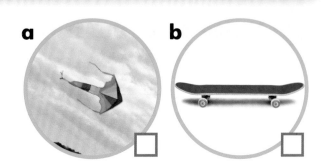

2 He loves playing tennis.

3 They like playing volleyball.

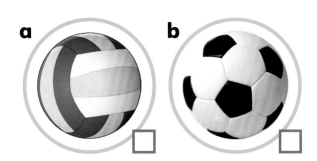

4 She likes climbing trees.

8 **Look at 7. Write the questions.**

1 _____

2 _____

3 _____

4 _____

9 **Label the body.**

bone   finger   foot
hand   muscle

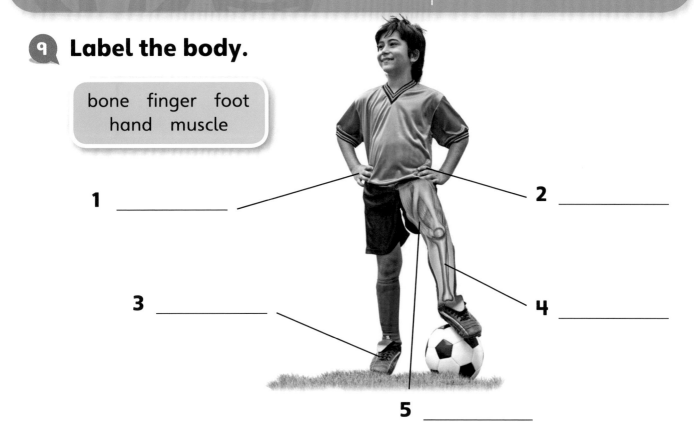

1 _____

2 _____

3 _____

4 _____

5 _____

10 **Listen, circle and match.**

We need to exercise every day. Exercise makes our **hands / muscles** strong. When we don't exercise, our bodies grow **big / weak**.

1 **Milk / Cake**, yoghurt and cheese help to make our **bones / feet** strong, too.

2 There are **27 / 70** bones in one hand. When we throw a ball, we use **43 / 34** muscles.

3 There are **20 / 26** bones in one foot. When we kick a ball, we use **13 / 30** muscles.

4 When we jump, we use more than **17 / 70** muscles.

a

b

c

d

11 **Look at 10. Circle T for true and F for false.**

1 Milk makes our bodies weak.   T   F

2 There aren't many bones in our hands.   T   F

3 We use muscles to help us jump.   T   F

4 We use muscles in our feet when we throw a ball.   T   F

5 We don't need to exercise every day.   T   F

6 When we kick a ball, we use our feet.   T   F

12 **Read and write.**

| Exercise   kick   move   throw   weak |

1 _____ makes our muscles strong.

2 When we don't exercise, our muscles grow _____.

3 When I jump, I _____ my body.

4 I _____ a ball with my foot.

5 I _____ a ball with my hands.

THINK BIG

What parts of our body do we use when ice skating? Tick (✓).

bones ☐   legs ☐   nose ☐

arms ☐   mouth ☐   muscles ☐

13 **Read and circle. Then match.** a

b

1 The children **doesn't / don't** like flying kites.

2 I **don't / doesn't** like climbing trees.

3 He **doesn't / don't** like playing tennis.

c

d

4 She **doesn't / don't** like doing gymnastics.

14 **Find and write the sentences.**

1 love dancing. We

_____

2 doesn't basketball. like She playing

_____

3 don't They exercising. like

_____

4 I skateboarding. love

_____

15 **Read and write too or neither.**

1 I love playing volleyball. Me, _____.

2 Hulya doesn't like riding bikes. Me _____.

3 We don't like skating. Me _____.

4 My brother loves playing football. Me, _____.

16 **Look at the pictures in 17. Read and circle.**

1 You play mancala with **stones** / **marbles**.

2 You **hit** / **catch** marbles with your finger.

3 You need a **ball** / **stone** to play jacks.

42
17 **Listen, read and match.**

1 Mancala is a game from Ghana. It's for two people.

2 In Guatemala, children play this game on their own or with friends.

3 In India, lots of people play this game together.

a You throw the ball, pick up the jacks, then catch the ball.

b You hit a marble with your finger. You win your friends' marbles.

c You move some stones around a board. You catch your friend's stones.

18 **Look at 17. Write marbles, jacks or mancala.**

1 Two people play this game. _____

2 You can play this game on your own. _____

3 You play this game with a board. _____

4 You hit them with your finger. _____

5 You throw and catch a ball. _____

19 **Read and write.**

ball   fingers   Guatemala   mancala   marbles   stones

1 In _____, children like playing jacks. They use a _____ and ten jacks.

2 In Ghana, children like playing _____. They use a board and some _____.

3 In India, children like playing _____. They use their _____.

THINK BIG

Circle. Which need a ball?

climbing   playing jacks   doing gymnastics

playing tennis   playing volleyball   riding a bike

running   skateboarding   swimming

20 **Read and match.**

1

a

Always wear a helmet and knee pads.

2

b

Always put one leg on each side.

3

c

Always sit down on the swing.

4

d

Always slide with your feet in front of you.

21 **Find and circle the letters ng and nk.**

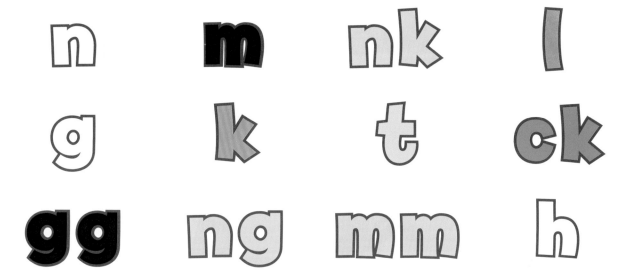

n   m   nk   l

g   k   t   ck

gg   ng   mm   h

22 **Read and circle the letters ng and nk.**

1 ring   **2** pink   **3** bang   **4** ink

23 **Match the words with the same sounds.**

1 wing   **a** sink

2 bank   **b** sing

24 **Listen and chant.**

Sing a song about a king.
Thank you! Thank you!
He's got a big pink ring
And big blue wings.
Thank you! Thank you!

Review

25 **Look and write.**

1 What does she love doing? She loves _____.

2 What _____ he like doing? He likes
_____.

3 What does he _____? He
_____.

4 What does she love _____? She
_____.

26 **Read and write.**

> bones   feet   hands   kick

1 We kick with our _____.

2 One hand has got 27 _____.

3 When we _____ a ball, we use 13 muscles.

4 We throw with our _____.

27 **Read and circle. Then ✓ or ✗ for you.**

1 I like playing volleyball.   **Me, too. / Me neither.** ☐

2 Elena doesn't like climbing trees.   **Me, too. / Me neither.** ☐

3 My mum hasn't got a skateboard.   **Me, too. / Me neither.** ☐

4 I love riding my bike.   **Me, too. / Me neither.** ☐

5 I don't like doing gymnastics.   **Me, too. / Me neither.** ☐

28 **Draw and write.**

What do you love doing?

I love _____.

In My House

1 **Look and write the names of the rooms. Then match.**

bathroom
bedroom
kitchen
living room

bed
chair
cupboard
dressing table
fridge
shelf
sofa
table
TV

2 **Look at 1. What's in the rooms? Write.**

1 There's a _____, a _____ and a _____ in the bedroom.

2 There's a _____, a _____ and a _____ in the living room.

3 There's a _____, a _____ and a _____ in the kitchen.

3 Listen and sing. Circle the pictures from the song.

Where Are My Keys?

Where are my keys, Mum?
Your keys are on the chair.
The chair? Which chair?
There are chairs everywhere!

There's a chair in the living room,
And one in the bedroom, too.
There are chairs in the dining room.
I don't know which chair. Do you?

Your keys are where you left them.
Put on your glasses and see.
They're on the chair behind you.
My keys are there! Silly me!

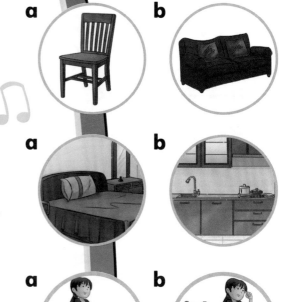

4 Look in your house. Count and write the number.

1 There are _____ chairs in the living room.

2 There are _____ chairs in the bedroom.

3 There are _____ chairs in the kitchen.

4 There are _____ chairs in the dining room.

Unit 3 31

5 **Read and circle.**

A Family Visit

These are my cousins. They're my aunt and uncle's children.

Where are your cousins now?

They're in the kitchen. Look!

Jamie, where's the TV?

It's in the living room.

1 The boys are Jamie's **brothers** / **cousins**.

2 The boys' mother is Jamie's **aunt** / **uncle**.

3 The boys are in the **bedroom** / **kitchen**.

4 The TV is in the **kitchen** / **living room**.

THINK BIG **Count and write the number.**

How many cousins have you got? ☐

How many aunts have you got? ☐

How many uncles have you got? ☐

6 **Read and match.**

1 in front of   **2** between   **3** next to   **4** behind

a    **b**   **c**   **d**

7 **Follow, write and circle.**

chair(x2)   kitchen   sofa

1 _____ the table?

_____ **next to / behind**

the _____.

2 _____ my keys?

_____ **in front of /**

behind the _____.

3 _____ his shoes?

_____ **on / between**

the _____.

4 _____ the cooker?

_____ **in / in front of**

the _____.

a

b

c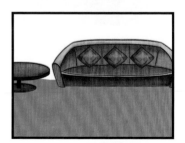

d

8 **Look and write. Use 's.**

1 Dan /

They're _____.

2 Suzie /

It's _____.

3 my mum /

It's _____.

4 her brother /

It's _____.

9 **Read the puzzles. Look at 8. Then write.**

1 It's behind the table, next to the chair. What is it?

_____

2 It's on the table, between the lamp and the bike. What is it?

_____

3 They're on the chair, behind the kite. What are they?

_____

4 It's on the dressing table, next to the backpack. What is it?

_____

10 **Write the names of the objects. Then write old or new.**

bike   computer   fridge   lamp   phone   TV

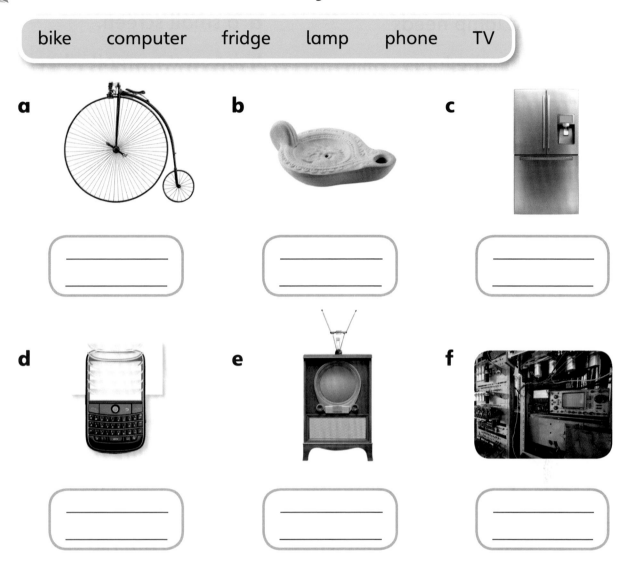

a

b

c

d

e

f

11 **Listen and read. Match to the old objects in 10.**

1 It's nearly 2,000 years old. It needs oil in it. The oil burns. ☐

2 Today we put them in our backpacks. But you can't put this one in your backpack. It needs a big room! ☐

3 It's very big and heavy but the screen is very small. ☐

4 It's got two wheels – a big wheel and a small wheel. When you ride it, you sit on the big wheel. It's fun! ☐

12 **Look at 11. Read and match.**

1 The old lamp needs   **a** a small screen.

2 The oil in the lamp   **b** has got a small wheel and a big wheel.

3 The old computer

     c oil.

4 You can't put the old computer

     d needs a big room.

5 The old TV has got   **e** in a backpack.

6 The old bike   **f** burns.

13 **Look, read and ✓.**

1 This bath is new. ☐   This bath is old. ☐

2 This jacket is new. ☐   This jacket is old. ☐

3 This is a new phone. ☐   This is an old phone. ☐

4 These are new skates. ☐   These are old skates. ☐

THINK BIG **Draw one old thing and one new thing in your house.**

14 Read and match.

1 I've got a dog. It's   **a** ours.

2 You've got a red pen. It's   **b** his.

3 My sister's got a new coat. It's   **c** theirs.

4 My brother's got a blue bike. It's   **d** mine.

5 The children have got a new ball. It's   **e** hers.

6 My friends and I have got some apples. They're   **f** yours.

15 Complete the table.

I	mine
you	1 _____
she	2 _____
he	3 _____
they	4 _____
we	5 _____

16 Read and write.

hers	His	Mine	our	Theirs	yours

1 **Teacher:** Are those red pens _____, Emma?
   Emma: No, they aren't. _____ are green.

2 **Teacher:** Have the boys got a pink ball?
   Girls: No, they haven't. _____ is red and white.
           We've got a pink ball. That's _____ ball.

3 **Teacher:** Is this Lucy's blue coat?
   Bella: No, it isn't _____. It's Peter's. _____
         coat is blue and Lucy's is purple.

17 **Read and match.**

1 You sit on a

2 You keep food cold in a

3 You sleep in a

4 You cook food in a

a bed.

b chair.

c cooker.

d fridge.

18 **Listen, write and match.**

Indonesia   Japan   Mali   Sudan

1 These people are sitting in a restaurant in _____ .

2 This is a clay pot. But in _____ , people don't cook food in them.

3 Some people in _____ don't sleep in beds.

4 Some people in _____ use a solar cooker.

a They keep food cold in them and they don't need electricity.

b It doesn't need fuel. It cooks food quickly in the sun.

c The chairs haven't got legs but they're very comfortable.

d They sleep in hammocks. When they don't need them, they put them in a cupboard.

19 **Look at 18 and write.**

cupboard   pot   restaurant   sun

1 The chairs are in a Japanese _____.

2 The clay _____ doesn't need electricity.

3 Some people in Indonesia keep their hammocks in a _____.

4 A solar cooker cooks food in the _____.

20 **Read and ✓.**

1 It needs electricity.   **a** a fridge ☐   **b** a clay pot in Sudan ☐

2 You keep it in a cupboard.   **a** a bed ☐   **b** a hammock ☐

3 It needs fuel.   **a** a solar cooker ☐   **b** a cooker ☐

4 It's got legs.   **a** my chair ☐   **b** a Japanese chair ☐

THINK BIG

Circle and write about your home.

In my kitchen, there **is / are** _____ and _____.

In my living room, there **is / are** _____ and _____.

Values | Be tidy.

21 **Listen and number. Then say.**

a

I put my dirty dishes in the sink.

b

I put my dirty clothes in the washing machine.

c

I put my toys in the toy box.

22 **Find and write the words.**

1 _____   xbo yot

2 _____   niks

3 _____   ngihsaw hcamein

23 **How do you keep your bedroom tidy? Draw and write.**

I _____.

24 **Find and circle the letters oo.**

25 **Read and circle the letters oo.**

1 moon   **2** book   **3** zoo   **4** foot

26 **Match the words with the same sounds.**

1 food   **a** look

2 good   **b** cool

27 **Listen and chant.**

Look in my
Cook book.
The food is good!
The food is cool!

28 Look and write.

bath   bed   chair   cooker   fridge   lamp   sink   TV

1 _____   2 _____   3 _____   4 _____

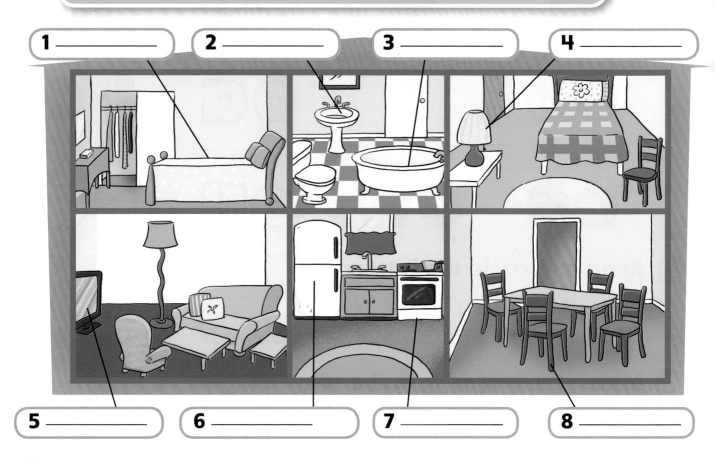

5 _____   6 _____   7 _____   8 _____

29 Look at 28. Match.

1 Where's the cooker?   a They're in the dining room.

2 Where's the bath?   b It's in the kitchen next to the sink.

3 Where are the chairs?   c It's in the bathroom.

30 Look at 28. Write.

1 What's in the bedroom?

There's a _____, a _____, a _____ and a _____

2 What's in the living room?

There's a _____, a _____, a _____ and a _____

31 **Look and write. Where is Milo?**

behind   between   in front of   next to

1 _____

2 _____

3 _____

4 _____

Let's play hide-and-seek!

32 **Look, read and circle.**

1 This computer is **old** / **new**.

2 These chairs are **old** / **new**.

3 This is an **old** / **new** phone.

4 These cars are **old** / **new**.

33 **Read and match.**

1 That bike is Marta's.

2 Bella's mum and dad have got a car.

3 Is this your toy?

4 It's Dan's skateboard.

5 These are our books.

a It's theirs.

b They're ours.

c It's hers.

d Yes, it's mine.

e It's his.

THINK BIG

1 **Look, find and number.**

2 **Look and find. Circle.**

At your school:
What do you like doing in the classroom? Circle one activity in red.

In your house:
What have you got in your bedroom? Circle one thing in blue.

3 **Think, look and draw.**

One thing is in the bedroom, in the classroom and in the playground. What is it?

MY CLASSROOM

1 cutting

2 gluing

3 using the computer

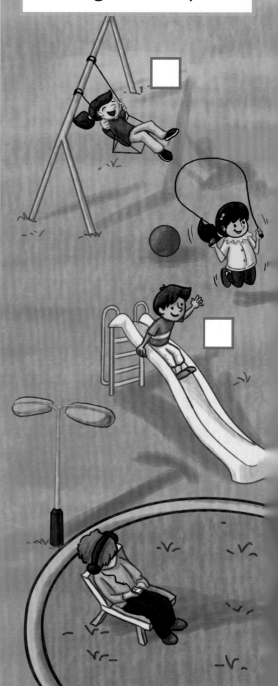

MY GAMES

4 playing on the seesaw

5 playing on the slide

6 playing on the swing

MY HOUSE

7 a bed

8 a dressing table

9 a lamp

unit 4 In My Town

1 **Look and match.**

1 shopping centre

2 train station

3 cinema

4 bank

5 restaurant

6 supermarket

a

b

c

d

e

f

2 Listen and sing. Circle the places on the map.

Maps Are Great!

Where's the bookshop?
I want to buy a book.
Here, I've got a map.
Come on. Let's take a look!

The bookshop is in River Street.
It isn't far from us.
Do you want to walk there?
No, thanks! Let's take the bus!

I want to send a letter, too.
Is there a post office? Do you know?

I'm looking at the map. Yes, there is.
It's near the bookshop. Come on. Let's go.

Maps are really great.
I use them every day.
In town or out of town
They help me find my way!

River Street
Maple Street
Bookshop
Train Station
Music Shop
Computer Shop
Main Street
Post Office
Park Street
Restaurant
Bus
Elm Street

3 What's in your town? Tick (✓).

☐ bookshop ☐ post office ☐ bus stop

☐ petrol station ☐ computer shop

4 Read and ✓.

Is There a Bookshop?

I want to buy a book. Is there a bookshop?

Yes, there is. Look!

I want to buy a computer game. Is there a computer shop?

Yes, there is. It's here.

I'm hungry. Let's eat first.

OK. There are restaurants over there!

What's in the shopping centre?

☐ There's a bookshop.

☐ There's a cinema.

☐ There's a computer shop.

☐ There are restaurants.

☐ There are supermarkets.

THINK BIG **What is there in your town? Read and circle.**

bank   bus stop   computer shop

petrol station   shopping centre

train station

5 **Look and write want to or wants to.**

me   Amy   Lisa   my brother

1 I _____ eat pizza.

2 Amy _____ go to the supermarket.

3 Lisa _____ buy a computer.

4 My brother _____ send a letter.

6 **Write.**

the bookshop, the cinema

the petrol station, the bank

I want to go _____ _____.

I _____ _____.

Mum wants to _____ _____.

She _____ _____.

7 **Draw a post office and a bookshop.**

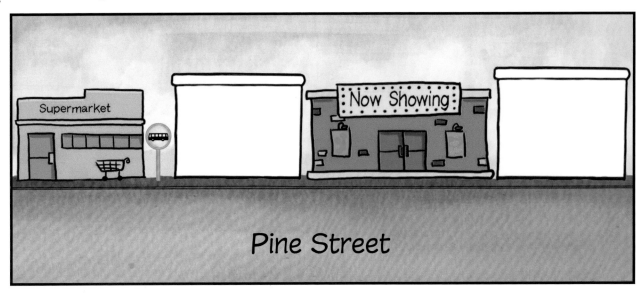

8 **Look at 7. Write Yes, there is or No, there isn't.**

1 Is there a bus stop in Pine Street?

_____

2 Is there a train station in Pine Street?

_____

3 Is there a supermarket next to the post office?

_____

4 Is there a cinema between the post office and the bookshop?

_____

5 Is there a petrol station near the bus stop?

_____

6 Is there a restaurant next to the cinema?

_____

9 **Look, read and write.**

bike   boat   bus   train

1 In London, some children go to school by  _____.

2 In Mexico City, many children go to school by  _____.

3 In Bangkok, many children go to school by  _____.

4 In Beijing, many children go to school by  _____.

10 **Listen, read and write.**

bike   canals   fast   underground   without

 There are lots of ¹_____ in Bangkok. Sunan goes to school by boat.

Lars and his friends live in Amsterdam. They go to school by ²_____ on bike streets. Bike streets are safe roads ³_____ cars.

 In Mexico City, there are lots of cars on the roads. Carmen goes to school by bus because it's ⁴_____. Her school is near a bus stop.

Sophia goes to school by ⁵_____. There are 468 underground stations in New York! Sophia's flat is near a station.

11 **Look at 10. Circle T for true and F for false.**

1 Sunan goes to school by car.   **T**   **F**

2 Cars don't go on bike streets in Amsterdam.   **T**   **F**

3 Carmen's school isn't near a bus stop.   **T**   **F**

4 Sophia lives near an underground station.   **T**   **F**

5 There are four hundred and eighty-six
   underground stations in New York.   **T**   **F**

12 **Read and write.**

| Amsterdam | Bangkok | Mexico City | New York |

1 There are lots of cars on the streets.   _____

2 There are lots of canals.   _____

3 There are safe bike streets.   _____

4 There are lots of underground stations.   _____

THINK BIG **How do teachers go to school in your country? Tick (✓).**

boat ☐   train ☐   bus ☐

bike ☐   car ☐

13 **Read and circle.**

1 How much **is / are** those sandwiches?

2 How much **is / are** that banana?

3 How much **is / are** that bike?

4 How much **is / are** that pizza?

5 How much **is / are** those books?

6 How much **is / are** the toys?

14 **Write the numbers.**

1 five euros and twenty-five cents   € _____

2 two euros and ninety-nine cents   € _____

3 sixty-eight cents   _____ c

4 ten euros   € _____

5 one euro and seventy-two cents   € _____

15 **Listen and match.**

1 €2.80   2 75c   3 €3.50   4 €12.99

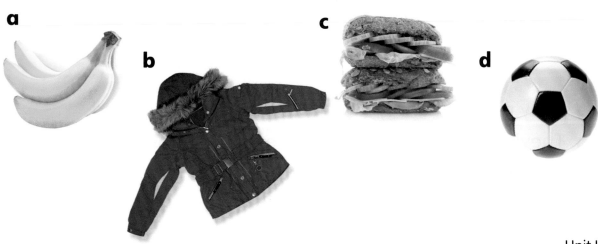

a   b   c   d

16 **Read and write.**

big   modern   new   slow

1 It isn't old. It's _____.

2 It isn't fast. It's _____.

3 It isn't small. It's _____.

4 It isn't from a long time ago. It's _____.

17 89 **Listen and read. Then circle and match.**

1 In Havana, some taxis are **old** / **new**. New taxis are black and yellow.

2 In London, taxis have a **colourful** / **famous** design.

3 In Berlin, most taxis look the **same** / **cheap**.

4 Tuk tuks in New Delhi have got three wheels. They're **cheap** / **fast**.

a They're green and yellow and they're easy to find.

b They're light brown and they're comfortable.

c They've got three wheels and they're fun to ride in.

d They look like cars from a long time ago. They're big and black.

18 **Look at 17 and match. Taxi words can be matched to more than one city.**

new

three wheels

black and yellow

fun

big and black

cheap

green and yellow

Havana

New Delhi

Berlin

London

modern

comfortable

light brown

easy to find

famous design

look the same

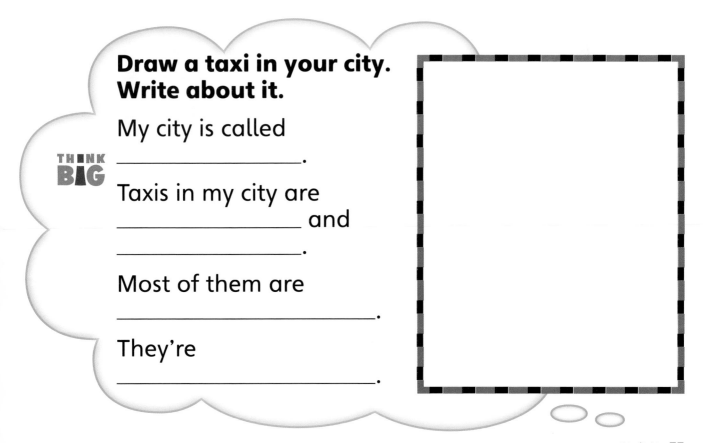

THINK BIG

Draw a taxi in your city. Write about it.

My city is called
_____.

Taxis in my city are
_____ and
_____.

Most of them are
_____.

They're
_____.

19 **Read, look and circle.**

a

1 I **look / don't** look left, then right, then left again before I cross the road.

b

2 I wait for the **blue / green** man.

c

3 I **always / never** cross at the pedestrian crossing.

20 **Find and write the words.**

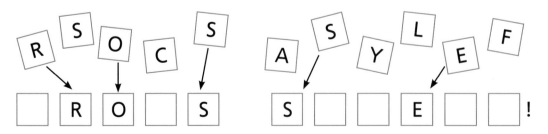

	R	O		S		S			E		

R O S S E !

21 **Find and circle the letters ai and oa.**

22 **Read and circle the letters ai and oa.**

1 rain   **2** coat   **3** train   **4** boat

23 **Match the words with the same sounds.**

1 road   **a** wait
2 tail   **b** soap

24 **Listen and write the letters. Then chant.**

95

Wear a c_____ t

To s_____ l the b_____ t!

Drive the tr_____ n,

In the r_____ n!

96
25 Listen and follow the path.

26 Look at 25. Write.

Where do they go?

1 _____

2 _____

3 _____

4 _____

5 _____

27 **Write want to or wants to. Then match.**

1 We _____ buy fruit.

2 She _____ go by train.

3 You _____ go to the bank.

4 He _____ buy petrol.

a There's a bank in Elm Street.

b Is there a petrol station near here?

c There's a supermarket behind the shopping centre.

d Is there a train station in London Road?

28 **Look, read and circle.**

1 In Mexico City, many children go to school by **bus** / **boat**.

2 In China, many children go to school by **train** / **bike**.

3 In London, many children go to school by **boat** / **train**.

4 In Bangkok, many children go to school by **boat** / **bike**.

29 **Read and circle.**

1 How much **is** / **are** those games?   They're / It's €5.

2 How much **is** / **are** that skateboard?   They're / It's €12.99.

3 How much **is** / **are** those apples?   They're / It's 45c.

4 How much **is** / **are** that hat?   They're / It's €2.85.

unit 5 My Dream Job

1 **Circle and match.**

a	p	e	o	c	k	a
d	s	i	n	g	e	r
o	p	b	l	d	w	t
c	i	v	r	o	t	i
t	s	i	e	d	t	s
o	v	p	r	t	s	t
r	h	a	c	t	o	r

pilot

artist

singer

actor

vet

doctor

2 **Look and circle.**

1 chef / writer

2 athlete / dancer

actor

pilot

Hey, What Do You Want to Be?

Hey, what do you want to be?
You have to choose just one.
There are so many different jobs.
I want one that is fun!

I want to be a ¹_____
And an athlete, too.
Or maybe a ²_____.
What about you?

I want to be an ³_____,
And I want to be a vet.
I want to be a ⁴_____, too.
Then I can fly a jet!

Chorus

dancer

5+5= 10

teacher

4 **Write and draw.**

I want to be **a / an**
_____.

5 **Read and circle.**

1 Jenny wants to be a **singer** / **writer**.

2 Dan wants to be a **writer** / **singer**.

3 Jenny and Dan are talking to their **friend** / **teacher**.

6 **Read the story again. What do they like doing? Match.**

1 eating

2 dancing

3 singing

4 writing

 Read and circle. I like music. I want to be a _____ and a _____.

chef   dancer   singer   writer

7 **Look and write.**

drawing   flying   singing   writing

1

What do you want to be?

I _____ to be a singer.
I like _____.

2

What do you want to be?

_____ an artist.
I like _____.

3

What do you want to be?

_____ a pilot. I _____.

4

What do you want to be?

_____
_____

8 **What do you like doing? Write and draw.**

I like _____
_____.

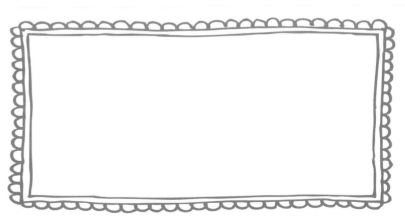

9 Look and write.

1

_____?

She wants to be a dancer.

2

_____?

He wants to be a teacher.

3

_____?

She wants to be a doctor.

4

_____?

He wants to be an athlete.

10 Look and match. Then write.

cooking	running

1 What does he want to be?

a She wants to be a chef.
She likes _____.

2 What does she want to be?

b He wants to be an athlete.
He likes _____.

11 Write. What do you want to be? Why?

_____

_____

_____

12 **Look and write.**

farmer   hairdresser   waiter

1 _____ 2 _____ 3 _____

13 **Read and write. Then listen and check.**

cuts   entertains   grows   makes   sells   takes

Goods are products. People produce goods: a farmer
¹_____ food and a carpenter ²_____ a table.
People also buy and sell goods. Food, books, clothes and
houses are goods. Electronic books that you can read on a
tablet are virtual goods.

Some people don't produce goods. They provide services.
A hairdresser ³_____ your hair. A singer or actor
⁴_____ you. These are services.

A restaurant provides goods and services. It ⁵_____
goods (food and drink). It also provides a service when the
waiter ⁶_____ the food to the tables.

14 **Look at 13 and circle.**

1 Goods are **services** / **products**.

2 When a carpenter makes a table, he's **providing a service** / **producing goods**.

3 An electronic book is a **product** / **service**.

4 When singers entertain you, they're **providing a service** / **selling a product**.

5 Restaurants provide **services** / **goods** / **services and goods**.

6 A waiter **sells products** / **provides a service**.

15 **Write goods or services.**

singer

food

doctor

cars

1 _____

2 _____

3 _____

4 _____

Read, guess and write. | chef   nurse   pilot

I look after ill people. Who am I? _____

I fly a plane. Who am I? _____

I cook food in a restaurant. Who am I? _____

16 **Read and match.**

1 I want to be a singer

2 I'm at the post office

3 I want to be an artist   **because**

4 I'm at the hairdresser's

5 I want to buy this
   T-shirt

a it looks nice.

b I like painting pictures.

c I like entertaining
   people.

d I want to post a letter.

e I need a new hairstyle.

17 **Read and circle.**

1 Let's go for a ride in that boat. It looks **tired / fun**.

2 Go to bed. You look **nice / tired**.

3 I want to read this book because it looks **good / kind**.

4 It looks **sunny / funny** outside. Let's go to the park.

5 Your new hairstyle looks **ill / nice**.

6 Go to the doctor. You look **happy / ill**.

18 **Read and write. Use look or looks.**

> cold   hot   ill   kind

1 I don't want to swim in the sea. It _____.

2 Are you OK? You _____.

3 I think that woman is a teacher. She _____.

4 Be careful! That oil _____.

19 **Match.**

1 scuba   **a** ranger

2 park   **b** rider

3 rodeo   **c** diver

20 **Listen and read. Match, then write the jobs from 19.**

1 Katie wants to be a vet one day. She lives with her family in Oklahoma, in the United States.

☐ _____

2 Juma lives in Botswana, Africa. Many animals are in danger there.

☐ _____

3 José Antonio lives in Costa Rica near the sea. His mum is a photographer.

☐ _____

a She loves the animals. She wants to help protect them one day. That's her father's job.

b He loves swimming. Sometimes he takes photos of the colourful fish under the water.

c They've got lots of cows and horses because they live on a ranch. She loves riding the horses.

21 **Look at 20. Circle T for true and F for false.**

1 Katie doesn't like the horses.   T   F

2 The animals on the ranch are in danger.   T   F

3 Juma's father is a park ranger.   T   F

4 Juma doesn't want to work with animals one day.   T   F

5 José Antonio loves taking photos of fish.   T   F

6 José Antonio's mother is a scuba diver.   T   F

22 **Read and write.**

| Botswana | colourful fish | horses and cows |
| in danger | the United States | underwater camera |

1 There are lots of _____ in the sea.

2 Some wild animals in Africa are _____.

3 There are _____ on a ranch.

4 Juma's home is in _____.

5 José Antonio uses his mum's _____.

6 Oklahoma is in _____.

THINK BIG

Which jobs would you like to try?
Put a ✓ or a ✗.

pilot ☐ doctor ☐ teacher ☐ scuba diver ☐

nurse ☐ vet ☐ writer ☐ rodeo rider ☐

mechanic ☐ park ranger ☐

hairdresser ☐ farmer ☐

23 Look, write and match.

1 I like Art.

a

I want to be a

_____.

2 I like Science.

b

I want to be an

_____.

3 I like Maths.

c

I want to be a

_____.

4 I like Music.

d

I want to be a

_____.

24 Find and write the sentences.

1 Maths. I like _____

2 I be to a want teacher. _____

3 I Art. like _____

4 writer. want a to be I _____

25 **Find and circle the letters ar, er and or.**

26 **Read and circle the letters ar, er and or.**

1 arm   **2** corn   **3** teacher   **4** car

27 **Match the words with the same sounds.**

1 singer   **a** for

2 born   **b** art

3 cart   **c** letter

28 **Listen and write the letters. Then chant.**
116

I want to be a sing _____

_____ an artist painting _____t.

I want to be a teach _____

Or a farmer with a c_____t!

29 Look and write. What do they want to be?

actor	artist	dancer	doctor
pilot	singer	teacher	vet

ACROSS →

1    4    7    8

DOWN ↓

2    3    5    6

30 **Look and write.**

1 What does she want to be?

_____

2 What does he want to be?

_____

3 What does she want to be?

_____

4 What does he want to be?

_____

31 **Complete the sentences with your own ideas. Use because.**

1 I want to be a writer _____

_____.

2 I want to be a park ranger _____

_____.

My Day

1 Listen and ✓. Then write.

1 a  **b**  □ □

2 a  **b** 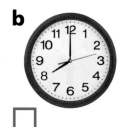 □ □

_____

3 a  **b**  □ □

4 a  **b**   □ □

_____

2 Read, draw and say.

1

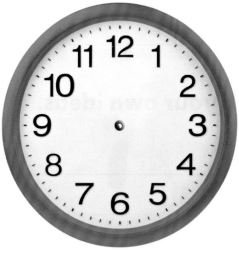

one o'clock

2

ten o'clock

3 Listen and sing. Look at the pictures. Then number in order.

a

b

What Time Is It?

Tick, tock. It's seven o'clock.
Time to get up and get dressed.
I want to stay in bed.
But it's time to brush my teeth!

Tick, tock. It's eight o'clock.
At nine o'clock I start school.
I eat my breakfast and get my books.
I love school, it's cool!

Tick, tock. It's three o'clock.
There's no more school today.
I do my homework and I go out.
And there's my friend to play.

c

d

Now it's evening and it's eight o'clock
And it's time to go to bed.
I watch TV and read my book.
Time to sleep now, good night!

4 Look at 3. Write.

1 I get up at _____.

2 I start school at _____.

3 I go out at _____.

4 I go to bed at _____.

5 **Read. Then write in order.**

Max gets up at two o'clock in the afternoon. Then he eats and goes out.

When does Max come back?

He comes back at seven o'clock. Then he sleeps again.

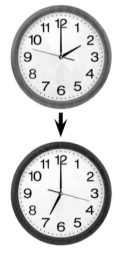

1 _____

2 _____

3 _____

4 _____

5 _____

Max comes home.

Max eats.

Max gets up.

Max goes out.

Max sleeps again.

THINK BIG

How many hours do I sleep?

I go to bed at _____ in the evening.

I get up at _____ in the morning.

I sleep for _____ hours.

6 **Listen and write.**

1 (get up: _____) **2** (start school: _____)

3 (finish school: _____) **4** (go out: _____)

5 (watch TV: _____) **6** (go to bed: _____)

7 **Look at 6. Write.**

1 When do you get up?

2 When ____ you start school?

3 When _____ finish school?

4 _____ go out?

5 _____ TV?

6 _____

1 I get up at _____.

2 I _____ at _____.

3 I _____ at _____.

4 _____ at _____.

5 _____

6 _____

8 Read and circle. Then draw and write the time.

1 When **do / does** she go out?
She **go out / goes out** at 4:00.

_____

2 When **do / does** he watch TV?
He **watch / watches** TV at 5:00.

_____

3 When **do / does** you go to bed?
I **go to bed / goes to bed** at 8:00.

_____

4 When **do / does** they get up?
They **get up / gets up** at 7:00.

_____

5 When **do / does** this film start?
It **start / starts** at 10:00.

_____

6 When **do / does** this film finish?
It **finish / finishes** at 12:00.

_____

9 **Are these ways to tell the time new or old?**
Write new or old.

1 candle clock _____

2 clock _____

3 hourglass _____

4 phone _____

5 sundial _____

6 water clock _____

7 watch _____

10 **Read and write. Then listen and check.**

| candle | cups | height | hourglass | Sand | shadow | sundial | water |

This is a ¹_____ clock. When it burns, it gets shorter. The ²_____ of the candle tells you the time. You can use this clock in the day or night.

An ³_____ uses sand to tell the time. ⁴_____ falls from the top to the bottom.

A ⁵_____ clock uses water to tell the time. It works like an hourglass. It's got two ⁶_____. The water falls from one cup to the other.

A ⁷_____ uses the sun to tell the time. The sun makes a shadow on the sundial. The ⁸_____ tells the time.

11 **Look at 10 and match.**

1 A candle tells the time when it   **a** sand.

2 The candle clock works in   **b** water.

3 The sundial needs   **c** burns.

4 An hourglass uses   **d** the day or night.

5 A water clock uses   **e** the sun.

12 **Look at 10. Circle T for true and F for false.**

1 A water clock doesn't work at night.   **T**   **F**

2 An hourglass uses a candle to tell the time.   **T**   **F**

3 The shadow tells you the time on a sundial.   **T**   **F**

4 A candle clock doesn't work in the sun.   **T**   **F**

5 A water clock has got two glasses for the water.   **T**   **F**

Write the times.

THINK BIG

2:00   3:00   **1**   10:00 _____   **2**   _____ 7:00

13 **Read and match.**

1 Where

2 Who

3 What

4 When

5 How

6 How many

a is your favourite game?

b do you get up?

c children are there in your class?

d does your teacher get to school?

e are your best friends?

f do you live?

Twenty-five.

It's basketball!

Near the school.

At seven o'clock.

Eva and Rob.

By bus.

14 **Find and write the sentences**

1 your work? does Where dad

_____

2 start? the When party does

_____

3 spell you How name? do your

_____

15 **Look and write. Use do, does, is or are.**

1 What _____ you like to do in your free time?

2 Who _____ your English teacher?

3 When _____ the film finish?

4 How many chairs _____ in your classroom?

5 Where _____ your grandparents live?

6 How _____ an hourglass work?

16 **Read and complete.**

| go | have | play | start | watch |

1 We _____ lunch at 7 o'clock.

2 We _____ school at 8 o'clock.

3 We _____ home after school.

4 I _____ TV at 6 o'clock.

5 I _____ games with my friends.

132

17 **Listen, read and write.**

| 5 o'clock | 8 o'clock | 9 o'clock | 10 o'clock | 12 o'clock | two | Sunday |

Bruno lives in Brazil. He goes to school from 7 o'clock to ¹_____. In the afternoon, he goes to a dance class. He has dinner at ²_____.

Jun lives in China. Her school starts at 8 o'clock and finishes at ³_____. They have a break for ⁴_____ hours at lunch time. After dinner, Jun does homework, then she watches TV.

Ali lives in Egypt. He goes to school from ⁵_____ to Thursday because Friday is a holiday. Classes start at 8 o'clock. At ⁶_____ they have a break and school finishes at 3 o'clock. After school, he plays with his sisters, then goes to bed at ⁷_____.

18 **Look at 17 and circle.**

1 Bruno goes to school for **four / five** hours.

2 He goes to a dance class **at / after** school.

3 Jun has a break at **lunch / dinner** time.

4 Jun watches TV **after / before** dinner.

5 Ali doesn't go to school on **Thursday / Friday**.

6 Ali **plays / goes to bed** at 9 o'clock.

19 **Read and write Bruno, Jun or Ali.**

1 _____ likes to dance.

2 _____ and _____ start school at 8 o'clock.

3 _____ finishes school at 12 o'clock

4 _____ has dinner at 8 o'clock.

5 _____ finishes school at 5 o'clock.

6 _____ likes watching TV.

Write the times for you.

I get up at _____.

I go to school from _____ to _____.

I have a break at _____.

I have lunch at _____.

I have dinner at _____.

I go to bed at _____.

20 **School starts at 8:00. Help Anna get to school on time. Follow the paths and choose 😊 or ☹.**

a

She gets up at six o'clock.　　She eats breakfast at seven o'clock.　　She gets to school at eight o'clock.

b

She gets her backpack ready the night before school.　　She brushes her teeth at nine o'clock.　　She gets to school at ten o'clock.

21 **How do you get to school on time? Tick (✓) and draw one step.**

☐ I get up early on school days.

☐ I get dressed quickly and eat breakfast.

☐ I get my backpack ready the night before school.

☐ I always get to school on time.

22 Find and circle the letters ch, tch and sh.

23 Read and circle the letters ch, tch and sh.

1 ship 2 chin 3 witch 4 fish 5 rich

24 Match the words with the same sounds.

1 match   a shop
2 chip   b watch
3 dish   c lunch

25 Listen and write the letters. Then chant.

Watch the wi ____,
She's having lun ____!
Fi ____ and ____ ips,
At the ____ op!

Review

26 **Write the words. Then colour the times.**

> brushes – **green**   finishes – **brown**   o'clock – **orange**
> school – blue   six – **purple**   snack – **red**

1 I start _____ at nine o'clock.

2 He _____ his teeth at eight o'clock.

3 The film _____ at five o'clock.

4 They eat a _____ at four o'clock.

5 She reads a book at seven _____.

6 I eat chicken and salad at _____ o'clock.

27 **Look and write.**

1 When _____ they go out?

They _____ at _____.

2 When _____ she get up?

She _____ at _____.

3 When _____ he start school?

He _____ at _____.

28 **Write about you. Add the times.**

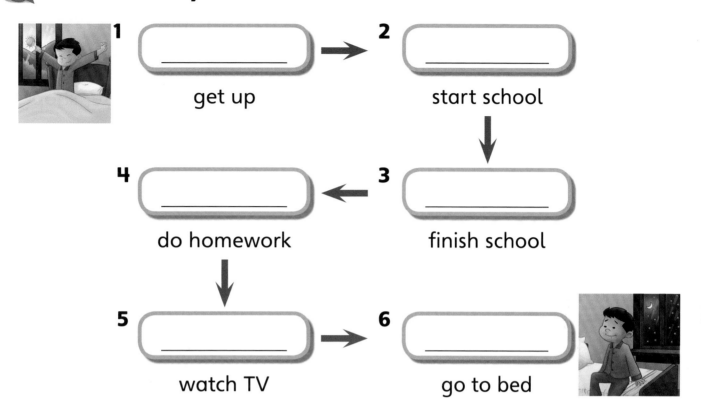

1 _____ get up → 2 _____ start school

4 _____ do homework ← 3 _____ finish school

5 _____ watch TV → 6 _____ go to bed

29 **Circle. Then write answers for you.**

1 **How** / **When** do you have breakfast?

_____

2 **What** / **Who** is your favourite colour?

_____

3 What time **do** / **does** school finish?

_____

4 **How** / **What** do you do after school?

_____

5 How many books **do** / **does** you have in your bag today?

_____

6 What **does** / **is** your teacher's name?

_____

THINK BIG

1 **Look, find and number.**

MY TOWN

1 bus stop
2 computer shop
3 supermarket

2 **Mark is visiting a small town. What can he do? Look at the town and ✓.**

Mark's To-Do List
- [ ] buy a book
- [ ] go to a restaurant
- [ ] send a letter
- [ ] buy fruit
- [ ] watch a film

3 **Think and draw. In the town, there isn't a _____ .**

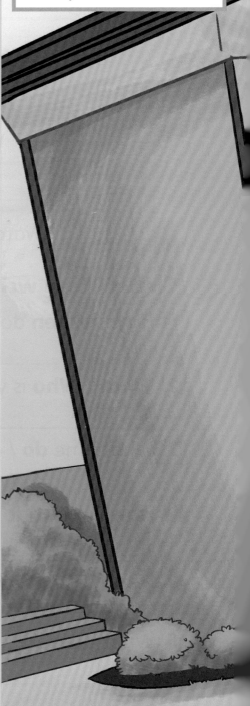

🔍 DREAM JOBS

4 artist

5 doctor

6 athlete

🔍 MY DAY

7 brush teeth

8 get up

9 go to bed

unit 7 My Favourite Food

1 **Look and match.**

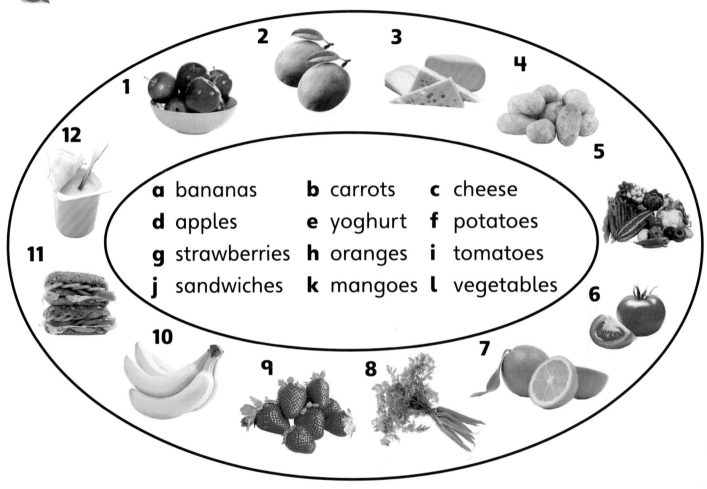

a bananas **b** carrots **c** cheese
d apples **e** yoghurt **f** potatoes
g strawberries **h** oranges **i** tomatoes
j sandwiches **k** mangoes **l** vegetables

2 **Look and write.**

I like _____ and _____ . I don't like _____ .

3 Listen and sing. Match and write.

a
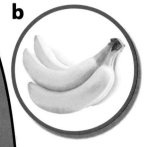
_____

b

_____

Let's Eat Lunch!

It's twelve o'clock.
Let's eat lunch.
Do you like bananas?
I like them for lunch!

Do you like tomatoes?
Yes, I do. I like tomatoes. I really do.
Do you like potatoes?
Yes, I do. I like potatoes, too.
Do you?

Meat and fruit,
Vegetables and snacks,
I like them all.
Can I have more please?

Have some chips
And a burger, too.
Let's share some ice cream.
I like eating lunch with you!

c
_____

d

_____

e
_____

f

4 Write and draw.

What do you want?

I want _____ .

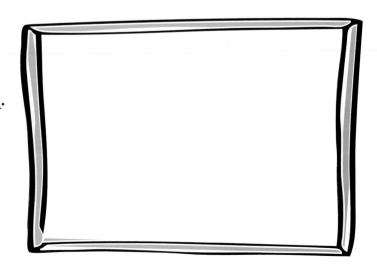

5 **Read. Then circle T for true and F for false.**

1 It's six o'clock.   **T**   **F**

2 Dan and Jamie want a snack.   **T**   **F**

3 Dan likes bananas.   **T**   **F**

4 Jamie doesn't like bananas.   **T**   **F**

5 Dan likes mangoes.   **T**   **F**

THINK BIG

Circle the fruit.

mangoes

bananas

carrots   oranges

apples

potatoes

meat

6 **What do you like? Listen and circle.**

1 a  b

2 a  b

3 a  b

4 a   b

7 **Look and write.**

1

I like _____

_____.

I don't like _____.

2

I like _____.

I don't like _____

_____.

3

I like _____

_____.

I don't like _____.

4

I like _____.

I don't like _____

_____.

8 Look and circle.

1

Do / Does she like strawberries?
Yes, she **do / does**.

2

Do / Does he like tomatoes?
No, he **don't / doesn't**.

3

Do / Does they like sandwiches?
Yes, they **do / does**.

4

Do / Does they like cheese?
No, they **don't / doesn't**.

9 Match. Then write.

1 Do you like meat?

a 😊 Yes, he _____.

2 Do they like vegetables?

b 😦 No, I _____.

3 Does he like burgers?

c 😊😊 Yes, they _____.

10 Are the snacks healthy or unhealthy? Put a ✓ or a ✗.

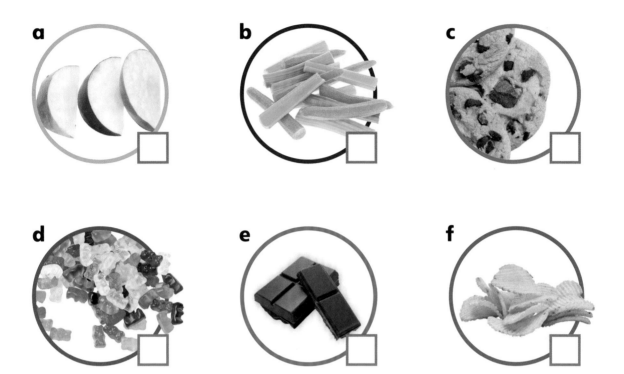

a

b

c

d

e

f

11 Read and write. Then listen and check.

152

| fat | healthy | labels | salt | Sugar | unhealthy |

Fruit and vegetables help us grow and keep us from getting ill. Some snacks are ¹_____ because they've got too much sugar, fat or salt in them.

²_____ in biscuits and sweets gives us energy but it makes us fatter. It's bad for our teeth and can give us diabetes.

Too much fat also makes us fatter. Too much fat and salt can give us heart disease. Chocolate has got lots of ³_____ in it and crisps have got lots of ⁴_____ in them.

Always read the ⁵_____ on snacks and choose only ⁶_____ ones.

12 **Look at 11 and circle.**

1 Too much **fruit** / **sugar** is unhealthy.

2 Biscuits and sweets give us **heart disease** / **energy**.

3 Too much sugar **keeps us from getting ill** / **makes us fatter**.

4 **Chocolate** / **Fruit** has got lots of fat in it.

5 **Crisps** / **Biscuits** can give us diabetes.

6 Healthy snacks **have** / **haven't** got too much sugar, salt or fat in them.

13 **Read and write sweets, biscuits, chocolate or crisps.**

1 There's too much salt in this snack.   _____

2 There's too much sugar in these snacks.   _____,

_____

3 There's too much fat in this snack.   _____

4 These snacks can give us diabetes.   _____,

_____

5 These snacks can give us heart disease.   _____,

_____

6 These snacks can make us fatter.   _____,

_____, _____, _____

 THINK BIG **Write about your favourite snack. Then circle.**

My favourite snack is _____.

It's **healthy** / **unhealthy**.

14 Can you count it? Put a ✓ or a ✗.

a
b
c
d

☐
☐
☐
☐

e
f
g
h

☐
☐
☐
☐

15 Look at 14. Write a, an or some.

1 _____ milk

2 _____ biscuit

3 _____ juice

4 _____ apple

5 _____ cheese

6 _____ fruit

7 _____ burger

8 _____ chocolate

16 Read and match.

1 There are some

a banana on the table.

2 There's a

b crisps on the plate.

3 There's an

c water in the glass.

4 There's some

d apple in the basket.

17 **Look and write.**

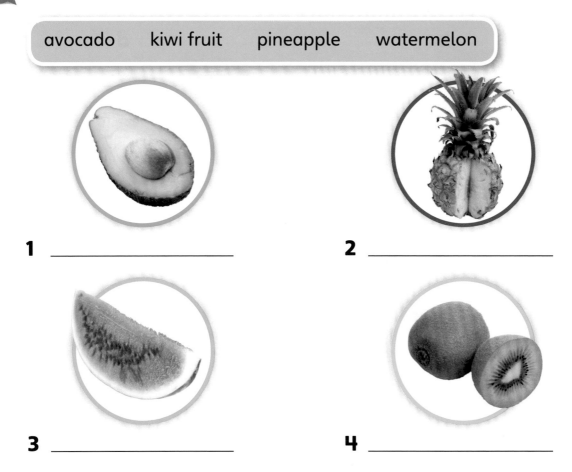

avocado   kiwi fruit   pineapple   watermelon

1 _____   2 _____

3 _____   4 _____

 18 **Read and circle. Then listen and check.**

They come from Mexico but also from lots of other countries. In Indonesia, people make a [1]**sweet / drink** with avocado, milk, sugar and sometimes chocolate.

They come from South Africa, Turkey, China and Japan. In Japan, some watermelons are [2]**square / sweet**!

They come from South America and the Philippines. In the Philippines, people make [3]**clothes / skin** from pineapple leaves.

They're ugly outside but [4]**beautiful / national** inside. They come from China but they now grow in many countries around the world.

19 **Look at 18. Circle T for true and F for false.**

1 Most watermelons are round.   T   F

2 You can make clothes from avocado leaves.   T   F

3 In Indonesia, they make a drink with kiwi fruit.   T   F

4 The pineapple is China's national fruit.   T   F

5 Watermelons grow in Turkey and South Africa.   T   F

6 Avocados come from Mexico.   T   F

20 **Read and write.**

Guess the fruit!

1 It's big. It's green on the outside and pink on the inside. What is it?   _____

2 It's yellow and it's got green leaves. What is it?   _____

3 It's green and it's got a very big seed inside. What is it?   _____

4 It's small and brown on the outside and green on the inside. What is it?   _____

THINK BIG **Draw your favourite fruit. Where does it come from?**

_____ is my favourite fruit.
It comes from _____. It's
_____ and _____.

21 **Look and circle.**

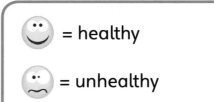

= healthy

= unhealthy

1

salad

2

crisps

3

biscuits

4

carrots

5

chocolate

6

apples

22 **Find and write the sentences.**

1 one   Just   please.   biscuit,

_____

2 thanks.   No   me,   crisps   for

_____

23 **Find and circle the letters ee and ie.**

24 **Read and circle the letters ee and ie.**

1 bee   **2** tie   **3** sheep   **4** pie

25 **Match the words with the same sounds.**

1 lie   **a** feet
2 see   **b** cried

26 **Listen and write the words. Then chant.**

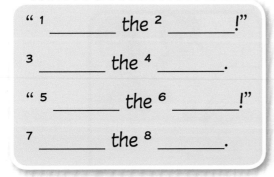

" **1** _____ the **2** _____!"

3 _____ the **4** _____.

" **5** _____ the **6** _____!"

7 _____ the **8** _____.

27 **What do you like? Look and write five foods.**

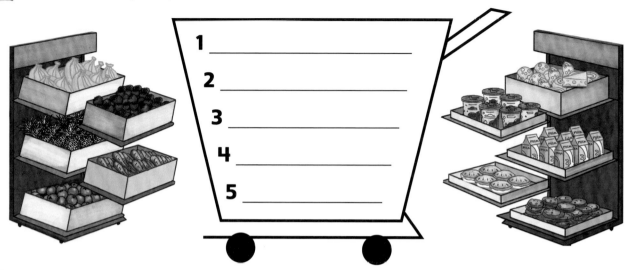

1 _____

2 _____

3 _____

4 _____

5 _____

28 **Look and write.**

1

Does she like bananas?

_____.

2

He _____ carrots.

He _____ cheese.

3

Does she like snacks?

_____.

She _____ meat.

4

They _____ cheese.

They _____

sandwiches.

29 **Look and write.**

	🍅	🥔	🍓	🍔
Anna	🙂	🙂	🙁	🙂
Ruben	🙁	🙂	🙁	🙂
Mary	🙂	🙁	🙂	🙂
You	○	○	○	○

🙂 = like

🙁 = doesn't like

1 _____ Anna _____ tomatoes?

_____

2 _____ Ruben _____ strawberries?

_____

3 _____ Mary _____ potatoes?

_____

4 _____ Mary and Ruben _____ burgers?

_____

5 _____ you _____ burgers?

_____

30 **Read and circle.**

1 Do you want **a** / **some** water?

2 There is **a** / **an** avocado tree in my garden.

3 Can I have **some** / **a** bananas, please?

4 I'm eating a burger and **a** / **some** chips.

5 There **is** / **are** some milk in the fridge.

6 There **is** / **are** two tomatoes on the table.

unit 8 Wild Animals

1 Look and write.

cheetahs   giraffes   hippos   kangaroos
monkeys   polar bears   zebras

ZOO

1 _____

2 _____

3 _____

4 _____

5 _____

6 _____

7 _____

2 Look and match.

1 crocodile   **2** parrot   **3** snake   **4** peacock

 a

 b

 c

 d

3 Listen and sing. Write the words.

kangaroo

To the Zoo!

I really like animals!
Do you like them, too?
That's why I'm so happy.
We're going to the zoo!

A **¹**_____ can jump.
A **²**_____ can jump, too.
Crocodiles can chase and swim.
And you, what can you do?

elephant

A **³**_____ can't fly or jump up high.
An **⁴**_____ can't climb trees.
Fish can't run and hippos can't fly.
Come and see them.
Oh, yes, please!

monkey

Now it's time to say goodbye
To every animal here.
But we can come back
And see them every year!

polar bear

4 What animals do you like seeing at the zoo?

_____ _____ _____

_____ _____ _____

5 **Read and circle.**

Monkeys Are Great!

Why do you like monkeys?

Monkeys are great! They can climb trees. They can jump.

So why do you like hippos?

A hippo has got a big mouth. It can eat a lot of food – like I can!

1 **Monkeys / Hippos** can climb trees.

2 **Monkeys / Hippos** can eat a lot of food.

3 **Monkeys / Hippos** can jump.

4 **Monkeys / Hippos** have got big mouths.

5 **Jamie / Jenny** can eat a lot.

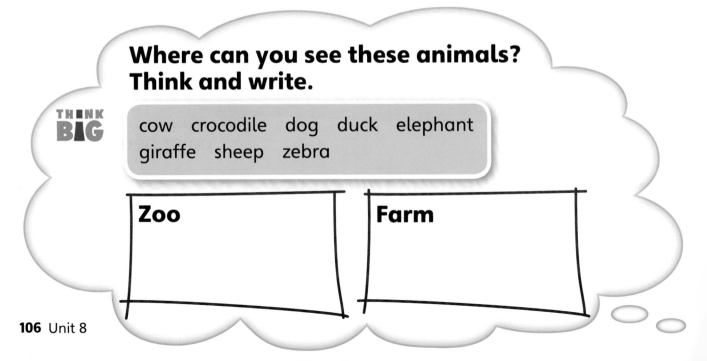

Where can you see these animals? Think and write.

THINK BIG

cow   crocodile   dog   duck   elephant
giraffe   sheep   zebra

Zoo	**Farm**

6 **Read and answer. Follow the correct path to the zoo.**

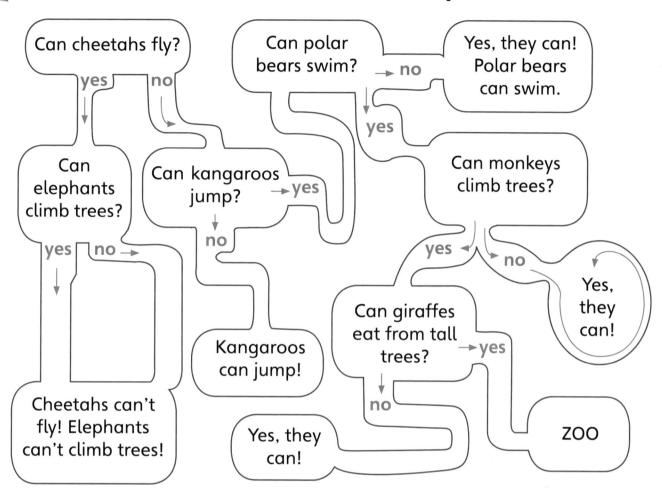

Can cheetahs fly?
yes   no

Can polar bears swim?   → no

Yes, they can! Polar bears can swim.
yes

Can elephants climb trees?

Can kangaroos jump?   → yes
no

Can monkeys climb trees?
yes   no

yes   no →

Yes, they can!

Can giraffes eat from tall trees?   → yes

yes
↓

Kangaroos can jump!

Cheetahs can't fly! Elephants can't climb trees!

no

Yes, they can!

ZOO

7 **Match and write. Use can or can't.**

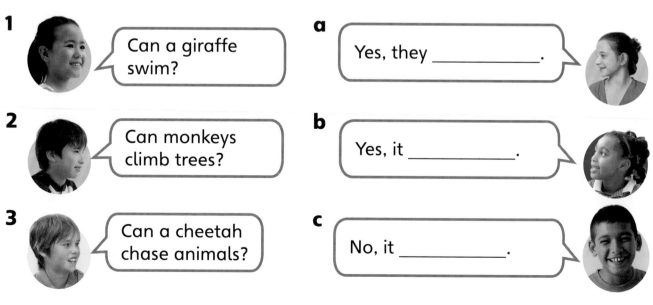

1   Can a giraffe swim?

a   Yes, they _____.

2   Can monkeys climb trees?

b   Yes, it _____.

3   Can a cheetah chase animals?

c   No, it _____.

8 **Look at the chart. Write questions and answers.**

	run	jump	climb trees	catch animals
1 giraffes	yes	no	no	no
2 polar bears	yes	yes	yes	yes
3 hippos	yes	no	no	no
4 cheetahs	yes	yes	yes	yes
5 zebras	yes	yes	no	no
6 kangaroos	no	yes	no	no

1 _____ run?

_____, they _____.

2 _____ jump?

_____, they _____.

3 _____ climb trees?

_____, they _____.

4 _____ catch animals?

_____, they _____.

5 _____ run?

_____, they _____.

6 _____ climb trees?

_____, they _____.

9 **Read and complete.**

> desert   forest   jungle   sea

1 Tigers live in the _____.

2 Fish live in the _____.

3 A lizard lives in the _____.

4 A deer lives in the _____.

10 **Listen, read and match.**

1 It's hot and it rains a lot. Monkeys, birds, butterflies and tigers live here.

2 It's cool and dark in the forest and there are lots of trees.

3 Lizards and snakes live here. There aren't many plants because it's very dry.

4 Water covers 71% of the planet. Many kinds of fish live in the oceans and seas.

a About 6% of the planet is desert.

b Deer, raccoons and foxes live here, too.

c Whales and seals also live in the salty water.

d The jungle covers only 2% of the planet but 50% of all plants and animals live here.

11 **Look at 10 and circle.**

1 It's **dry** / **cool** in the desert.

2 It's **hot** / **dry** in the jungle.

3 The ocean covers **17%** / **71%** of the planet.

4 Colourful birds live in the **desert** / **jungle**.

5 There are lots of trees and plants in the **desert** / **forest**.

12 **Look and write.**

1 _____ live in _____.

2 _____ live in _____.

3 _____ live in _____.

4 _____ live in _____.

THINK BIG **Circle the odd one out. Which animals live in the sea?**

fish   lizard   seal   shark   whale

13 **Complete the table.**

| beautiful | big | blue | brown | cold | long |
| new | nice | old | pink | small | square |

opinion	size/shape	age	colour

14 **Read and circle.**

1 You have a **red nice** / **nice red** bike.

2 My grandpa is **a kind old** / **an old kind** man.

3 Is this your **blue new** / **new blue** scarf?

4 A kiwi fruit is a **funny brown** / **brown funny** fruit.

5 That's a **black beautiful** / **beautiful black** bird.

15 **Look and write.**

1 It's a _____ _____ monkey. (brown / small)

2 Those are _____ _____ birds. (red / big)

3 There are lots of _____ _____ fish in the sea. (beautiful / round)

4 Look at that _____ _____ watermelon! (pink / square)

5 I have a(n) _____ _____ desk. (old / nice)

16 **Look and write.**

| koala | llama | snow monkey |

1 _____ 2 _____ 3 _____

17 **Read and write. Then listen and check.**

| forest | friendly | gum tree | jump | sleep | snowballs |

Angela lives in Peru with her llama, Papi. Papi isn't wild. He's a ¹ _____ pet and he can ² _____ high.

Kyoko lives in Japan. There are lots of snow monkeys in the ³ _____ near her home. They like to make ⁴ _____.

Vincent lives in Australia. There's a koala in the ⁵ _____ outside his window. Koalas are very slow. They ⁶ _____ and eat a lot.

18 **Look at 17 and circle.**

1 Angela's llama **is** / **isn't** wild.

2 Papi can **make snowballs** / **jump**.

3 Snow monkeys live in **Kyoko's garden** / **the forests**.

4 They are **wild** / **friendly**.

5 The koala **is** / **isn't** a pet.

6 It sleeps a lot **but** / **and** it eats a lot.

19 **Look at 17. Write the countries.**

1 Llamas come from _____.

2 Snow monkeys come from _____.

3 Koalas come from _____.

THINK BIG **Draw and write about your favourite animal for the Outside My Window website.**

This is a _____. It comes from _____.

It lives _____.

It _____.

It's my favourite animal because _____.

20 **Look, listen and write.**

1 I like peacocks.
They're so _____.

2 Monkeys are so
_____.

3 Giraffes are _____.
Their necks are so long.

4 Elephants are very
_____.

21 **Find and write the describing words.**

1 _____ z a a m n g i

2 _____ v r e e c l

3 _____ f l u t i u e b a

4 _____ o g n t s r

22 **Find and circle the letters ou and ow.**

23 **Read and circle the letters ou and ow.**

1 you   **2** owl   **3** soup   **4** cow

24 **Match the words with the same sounds.**

1 down   **a** route

2 group   **b** town

25 **Listen and write the words. Then chant.**

183

An ¹_____ went
²_____ to ³_____
To see a ⁴_____ of
⁵_____ drinking
⁶_____ .

26 **Look and write.**

ACROSS →

3   5   6

DOWN ↓

1   2   4

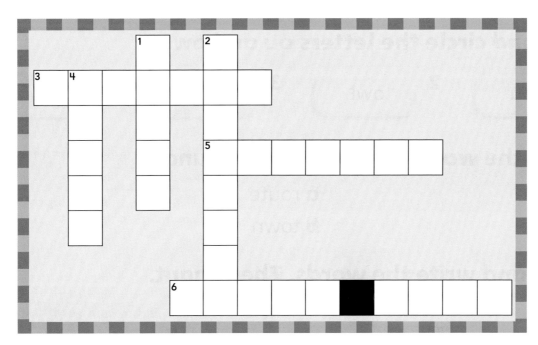

27 **Write. Then match questions and answers.**

1 _____ a monkey climb trees?

2 _____ parrots fly?

3 _____ a peacock swim?

4 _____ snakes run?

a No, they _____.

b Yes, it _____.

c Yes, they _____.

d No, it _____.

28 **Look and circle.**

1 elephant / hippo   **2 giraffe / crocodile**   **3 lizard / snake**

29 Read and write.

| deserts | forests | jungles | oceans |

1 Foxes live in _____.

2 Whales live in _____.

3 Lizards live in _____.

4 Monkeys live in _____.

30 Tick (✓) the correct sentences.

1 Papi is an old friendly llama. ☐

2 Koalas are small slow animals. ☐

3 Snow monkeys are wild beautiful animals. ☐

4 An elephant is a big grey animal. ☐

5 My pet is a small black and white dog. ☐

unit 9 Fun All Year

1 Number the months in order.

April
MON	TUE	WED	THU	FRI	SAT	SUN
1	2	3	4	5	6	7
8	9	10	11	12	13	14
15	16	17	18	19	20	21
22	23	24	25	26	27	28
29	30					

January
MON	TUE	WED	THU	FRI	SAT	SUN
1	2	3	4	5	6	7
8	9	10	11	12	13	14
15	16	17	18	19	20	21
22	23	24	25	26	27	28
29	30	31				

May
MON	TUE	WED	THU	FRI	SAT	SUN
				1	2	3	4	5
6	7	8	9	10	11	12
13	14	15	16	17	18	19
20	21	22	23	24	25	26
27	28	29	30	31		

August
MON	TUE	WED	THU	FRI	SAT	SUN
			1	2	3	4
5	6	7	8	9	10	11
12	13	14	15	16	17	18
19	20	21	22	23	24	25
26	27	28	29	30	31	

July
MON	TUE	WED	THU	FRI	SAT	SUN
1	2	3	4	5	6	7
8	9	10	11	12	13	14
15	16	17	18	19	20	21
22	23	24	25	26	27	28
29	30	31				

November
MON	TUE	WED	THU	FRI	SAT	SUN
			1	2	3	
4	5	6	7	8	9	10
11	12	13	14	15	16	17
18	19	20	21	22	23	24
25	26	27	28	29	30	

December
MON	TUE	WED	THU	FRI	SAT	SUN
						1
2	3	4	5	6	7	8
9	10	11	12	13	14	15
16	17	18	19	20	21	22
23	24	25	26	27	28	29
30	31					

June
MON	TUE	WED	THU	FRI	SAT	SUN
					1	2
3	4	5	6	7	8	9
10	11	12	13	14	15	16
17	18	19	20	21	22	23
24	25	26	27	28	29	30

October
MON	TUE	WED	THU	FRI	SAT	SUN
	1	2	3	4	5	6
7	8	9	10	11	12	13
14	15	16	17	18	19	20
21	22	23	24	25	26	27
28	29	30	31			

February
MON	TUE	WED	THU	FRI	SAT	SUN
			1	2	3	4
5	6	7	8	9	10	11
12	13	14	15	16	17	18
19	20	21	22	23	24	25
26	27	28				

March
MON	TUE	WED	THU	FRI	SAT	SUN
			1	2	3	
4	5	6	7	8	9	10
11	12	13	14	15	16	17
18	19	20	21	22	23	24
25	26	27	28	29	30	31

September
MON	TUE	WED	THU	FRI	SAT	SUN
						1
2	3	4	5	6	7	8
9	10	11	12	13	14	15
16	17	18	19	20	21	22
23	24	25	26	27	28	29
30						

2 Write the month.

1 This month has got five letters.

This month is before April.

_____

2 This month has got six letters.

This month is after July.

_____

3 This month has got eight letters.

This month is between October and December.

_____

3 Listen and chant. Then write.

I Like July!

¹_____ is my favourite month.
I like ²_____, too.
I'm happy and on holiday,
There is so much to do!

I also like ³_____.
That's when I start school.
I'm so excited, aren't you?
My friends will be there, too!

I don't like ⁴_____.
It is so very cold.
But then it is my birthday, too.
This year I'm eight years old!

August

July

December

September

4 What month do you like? Write. Then circle how many days it's got.

M	T	W	T	F	S	S
		1	2	3	4	5
6	7	8	9	10	11	12
13	14	15	16	17	18	19
20	21	22	23	24	25	26
27	28	29	30	31		

5 **Read and write.**

1 Jenny's favourite month is
_____.

2 Jenny _____ goes on
holiday in December.

3 Dan _____ goes on
holiday in winter.

4 It's too _____.

What do you do in December?

TH NK BIG

I always _____ in December.

I never _____ in December.

6 **Look at the calendar. Then write and circle.**

June

Mon	Tues	Wed	Thur	Fri	Sat	Sun
				1	2	3
4	5	6	7	8	9	Visit Cousins 10
11	12	13	14	Sally's party 15	16	17
Father's Day 18	19	20	21	22	23	Beach 24
25	26	27	28	29	30	

1 Do you have a New Year's party in June?

No, I _____ . I **always** / **never** have a New Year's party in June.

3 What do you celebrate in June?

We **always** / **never** celebrate Father's Day in June.

5 Do you go to the beach in June?

Yes, we _____ . We **always** / **never** go to the beach in June.

2 What do you do in June?

I **always** / **never** visit my cousins in June.

4 Do you have Billy's party in June?

No, we _____ . We **always** / **never** have his party in June.

7 **Answer about you. Write and circle.**

Do you go on holiday in June?

_____ , I _____ . I **always** / **never** go on holiday in June.

Language in Action

8 **Look and write always or never.**

Hi, I'm Julia. I always go ice skating in winter.

	winter	spring	summer	autumn
always	go ice skating	have a party	go to the beach	visit my cousins
never	ride my bike	go on holiday	go to school	celebrate New Year's

1 What does she do in winter?

She _____ rides her bike. She _____ goes ice skating.

2 What does she do in spring?

She _____ has a party. She _____ goes on holiday.

3 What does she do in summer?

She _____ goes to the beach. She _____ goes to school.

4 What does she do in autumn?

She _____ celebrates New Year's. She _____ visits her cousins.

9 **Choose a season. Then write.**

What do you do in _____?

I always _____. I never _____.

10 **Read and match for you.**

In my country,

1	February and March are	**a**	in spring.
2	May is	**b**	in summer.
3	July and August are	**c**	in autumn.
4	September and October are	**d**	in winter.

11 **Listen, circle and match.**

194

1 On May Day, children in England hold **wishes** / **ribbons** and dance around a **tree** / **pole**.

a

2 In February and March, there are carnivals in Italy. People throw small pieces of paper called **bamboo** / **confetti**.

b

3 The Mid-Autumn Festival in China happens when the **star** / **moon** is very big. Children wear **ribbons** / **masks** and eat mooncakes.

c

4 In summer, people in Japan celebrate the star festival, Tanabata. They **hang** / **wear** wishes on a bamboo **ribbon** / **wish** tree.

d

12 **Look at 11 and match.**

1 People celebrate May Day

2 On May Day, children dance

3 There are carnivals in Italy

4 At the carnival, children throw

5 At the Mid-Autumn Festival, children eat

6 At Tanabata, people hang wishes

a on a bamboo tree.

b confetti.

c mooncakes.

d around a pole.

e in February and March.

f in spring.

13 **Look at 11. Write the countries.**

1 In _____, people throw confetti.

2 In _____, people eat mooncakes.

3 In _____, people celebrate the star festival.

4 In _____, children put ribbons on a pole.

THINK BIG

What do people do at your favourite festival? Tick (✓) and write.

wear masks ☐   eat special food ☐   dance ☐
make wishes ☐   throw paper ☐

My favourite festival is called _____.

People _____

and _____.

14 **Read and match.**

What's the weather like?

1 It's cold.

2 It's snowing.

3 It's hot.

4 It's sunny.

5 It's raining.

a

b

c

d

e

15 **Look and read. Circle T for true and F for false.**

London, England	Paris, France	Mexico City, Mexico	New York, USA	Istanbul, Turkey	Tokyo, Japan	Shanghai, China	Rome, Italy

1 It's cold in London.   T   F

2 It's hot in Mexico City.   T   F

3 It's sunny and cold in Istanbul.   T   F

4 It isn't raining in Rome.   T   F

16 **Look at 15 and write.**

1 It's _____ in Paris.

2 It's _____ in New York.

3 It's _____ and _____ in Tokyo.

4 It's _____ and _____ in Shanghai.

17 **Look at the pictures in 18 and match. Write 1–3.**

soup ☐

grapes ☐

coal ☐

18 **Listen, read and match.**

198

1 At midnight on New Year's Eve in Scotland, people hold hands and sing a special song. Then they visit their family and friends.

2 In Japan, people eat a special noodle soup on New Year's Eve for good luck.

3 In Spain, people eat twelve grapes at midnight. They eat one grape for each chime of the clock.

a People think that the grapes bring good luck. Then there are fireworks.

b Then they listen to a bell ring 108 times at midnight.

c The first person through the door gives a piece of coal for good luck.

19 **Look at 18. Write Scotland, Japan or Spain.**

1 They listen to something. _____

2 They hold hands. _____

3 They eat fruit. _____

4 They have fireworks. _____

5 They eat soup. _____

6 They visit people. _____

20 **Read and match.**

1 How many grapes do they eat at midnight in Spain?

     a noodles

2 What happens after they eat the grapes?

     b 108

3 How many times does a bell ring at midnight in Japan?

     c fireworks

4 What do people believe brings good luck at New Year in Scotland?

     d 12

5 What is in the special New Year's soup in Japan?

     e a piece of coal

THINK BIG

What do you do on New Year's Eve?

On New Year's Eve, I _____

_____

_____.

21 Read, look and match.

1 In spring, he rides his bike.

a

2 In summer, she likes to swim in the sea.

b

3 In autumn, they rake leaves.

c

4 In winter, they skate on ice.

d

22 Find and write the words. Then match each season to the months in your country.

1 t n r e w i _____

2 r p s g n i _____

3 u t a n u m _____

4 m r e u s m _____

a December, January, February

b March, April, May

c June, July, August

d September, October, November

23 **Write the alphabet in the correct order.**

Aa ___ ___ __d ___ F_ ___ __h I_

Q_ ___ O_ ___ M_ ___ __k ___

___ __t ___ V_ ___ __x Y_ ___

24 **Listen and write the letters and words. Then chant.**

A, B, C, ¹____, E, ²____, G.
I can see an ant and a ³_____.
What can you see?
H, I, ⁴____, K, L, ⁵____, N, O, ⁶____.
I can see a ⁷_____ and some ink. What can you see?
Q, ⁸____, S, T, ⁹____, V.
I can see a ¹⁰_____ and a snake.
What can you ¹¹_____?
W, ¹²____, Y and ¹³____.
I can see ¹⁴_____ yellow wolves
and a ¹⁵_____, I said!

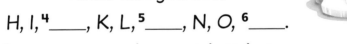

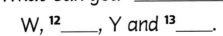

25 Follow the maze. Write the months in order.

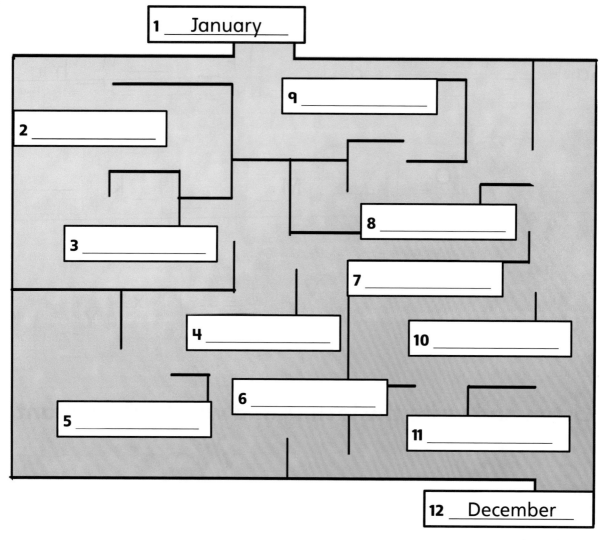

1 ___January___

2 _____

3 _____

4 _____

5 _____

6 _____

7 _____

8 _____

9 _____

10 _____

11 _____

12 ___December___

26 Complete the dialogue.

| always | Do | don't |
| never | What | |

Maria: ¹_____ do you do in winter?

Peter: We ²_____ go ice skating.

Maria: We always visit our cousins in winter. We ³_____ go ice skating.

Peter: ⁴_____ you go to the beach in summer?

Maria: No, we don't. We ⁵_____ go to the beach in summer. We always go to the swimming pool and eat ice cream!

27 Listen and circle. Then match.

1 They **always** / **never** have a New Year's party in winter.

2 He **always** / **never** goes on holiday in autumn.

3 I **always** / **never** swim in spring.

4 She **always** / **never** goes to school in summer.

a

b

c

d

28 Draw and write about you.

1 What do you always do in autumn?

_____

_____

What's the weather like?

_____

_____

2 What do you never do in spring?

_____

_____

What's the weather like?

_____

_____

1 **Look, find and number.** 🔍

2 **Look at 1 and write. Add one food word, one animal word and one month word.**

3 **Look at the table and circle one food in red:**

What do you like eating for lunch?

4 **Look at the table and circle one food in blue:**

What do you never eat for lunch?

5 **Think, look and circle in green.**

There's a hat on an elephant. That's silly. What other silly things can you see?

🔍 **FOOD**

1	carrots
2	cheese
3	bananas

🔍 ANIMALS

4 zebra

5 elephant

6 giraffe

_____

🔍 MONTHS

7 summer month

8 winter month

9 autumn month

_____

What**'s** he/she **doing**? He**'s**/She**'s writing**.

What **are** they **doing**? They**'re gluing**.

1 **Circle the correct form of the verb. Then match.**

1 What **is** / **are** he doing? **a** She's colouring.

2 What **is** / **are** they doing? **b** They're watching a DVD.

3 What **is** / **are** she doing? **c** He's counting.

How many pictures are there? **There's** one picture.

How many books are there? **There are** three books.

2 **Look and write. Use There's or There are.**

1 _____ one teacher.

2 _____ one book.

3 _____ three pupils.

> What **does** he/she **like doing**?   He/She **likes skateboarding**.
>
> What **do** they **like doing**?   They **like flying kites**.

1 **Circle the correct form of the verb.**

1 What **do / does** he like doing?

He **like / likes** playing tennis.

2 What **do / does** they like doing?

They **like / likes** climbing trees.

3 What **do / does** she like doing?

She **like / likes** doing gymnastics.

2 **Look and write the question. Then write the answer.**

listen   use

1

What _____ doing?

He _____ the computer.

2

What _____ doing?

They _____.

Where**'s** the TV?	**It's** on the table.
Where **are** the chairs?	**They're** in the living room.

1 **Look. Write Where's or Where are.**

1 _____ the keys?

2 _____ the phone?

3 _____ the football?

4 _____ the skates?

2 **Look at 1. Answer the questions.**

1 _____ in the bedroom.

2 _____ on the bed.

3 _____ in the bath.

4 _____ next to the chair.

My mum**'s** phone is on the dressing table.   Ben**'s** keys are on the table.

3 **Circle the correct word.**

1 Where are **Mum / Mum's** keys?

2 My **cousins / cousin's** are riding their bikes.

3 **Emily / Emily's** bedroom is next to the bathroom.

4 **Joes / Joe's** clothes are in the cupboard.

I/We/They/You **want to** send a letter.   He/She **wants to** go to the bank.

1 **Circle the correct form of the verb.**

1 I **want** / **wants** to buy a book.

2 My aunt and uncle **want** / **wants** to go to a computer shop.

3 Julia **want** / **wants** to send a letter.

4 He **want** / **wants** to eat.

Is there a post office near here?	Yes, **there is**.
Is there a bank in Elm Street?	No, **there isn't**.

2 **Look and write.**

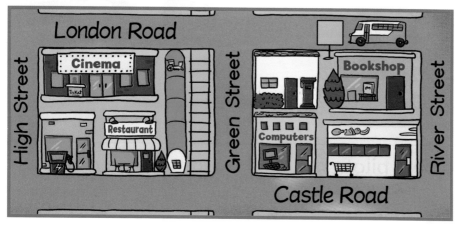

1 Is there a bookshop
in High Street?

_____

3 Where's the cinema?
_____ a cinema
near the train station?

_____

2 Is there a computer shop
in River Street?

_____

4 Let's eat. _____
a restaurant near here?
Yes, _____

| What **do** you **want to be**? | I **want to be** an actor. |
| What **does** he/she **want to be**? | He/She **wants to be** a doctor. |

① Look and write.

1

What does he want to be?

He _____.

2

What does she want to be?

She _____.

3

_____?

She wants to be a pilot.

4

_____?

He wants to be a chef.

5

_____?

He _____.

6

What do you want to be?

_____

When **does** he/she **get up**?	He/She **gets up** at 6:00.
When **do** you/they **go to** bed?	I/They **go to** bed at 8:00.
When **does** the film **start**?	It **starts** at 7:00.

1 **Look and match. Then write the questions and answers.**

 **1** When

2 When

	they go out?
do	she get up?
does	she go to bed?
	school finish?

 **3** When

4 When

1 _____?

_____

2 _____?

_____

3 _____?

_____

4 _____?

_____

Unit 7 | Extra Grammar Practice

Do you **like** fruit?	Yes, I **do**. I like apples and bananas. No, I **don't**. I like cheese.
Do they **like** vegetables?	Yes, they **do**. They like carrots and potatoes. No, they **don't**. They like fruit.
Does he/she **like** fruit?	Yes, he/she **does**. He/She likes mangoes and oranges. No, he/she **doesn't**. He/She likes yoghurt.

1 **Circle the correct form of the verb.**

1 **Do** / **Does** she like meat?

No, she **don't** / **doesn't**. She likes sandwiches.

2 **Do** / **Does** they like snacks?

Yes, they **do** / **does**.

3 **Do** / **Does** she like cheese?

Yes, she **do** / **does**.

4 **Do** / **Does** they like tomatoes?

No, they **don't** / **doesn't**. They like potatoes.

5 **Do** / **Does** you like strawberries?

Yes, I **do** / **does**. I love strawberries!

2 **Look and write the questions and answers.**

1 you	bananas	😕
2 Emma	oranges	😕
3 Sue and Hugo	vegetables	🙂

1 _____ you _____ bananas?   _____

2 _____ she _____ oranges?   _____

3 _____ they _____ vegetables?   _____

Can a kangaroo jump? Yes, it **can**.	**Can** a snake jump? No, it **can't**.
Can kangaroos jump? Yes, they **can**.	**Can** snakes jump? No, they **can't**.

1 **Read. Circle T for true and F for false.**

1 Cheetahs can run.   T   F

2 A giraffe can fly.   T   F

3 A polar bear can jump.   T   F

4 An elephant can eat meat.   T   F

5 Hippos can climb trees.   T   F

6 Kangaroos can swim.   T   F

2 **Look at 1. Correct the false sentences. Use can't.**

1 _____

2 _____

3 _____

4 _____

3 **Write the questions. Use the words. Then write the answer.**

chase   fly   talk   write

1 Can a cheetah _____ a zebra?   Yes, _____.

2 _____ a cheetah _____?   No, _____.

3 _____ cheetahs _____?   No, _____.

4 _____ cheetahs _____ their name? No, _____.

| What does he/she do in January? | He/She **always** has a New Year's party in January. |
| Do you go on holiday in winter? | No, I/we don't. I/We **never** go on holiday in winter. |

1 **Answer the questions about you. Circle the words.**

1 Do you do homework at six o'clock?

Yes / No. I **always** / **never** do homework at six o'clock.

2 Does your father like reading books?

Yes / No. He **always** / **never** reads books.

3 Do you like playing games at school?

Yes / No. I **always** / **never** play games at school.

4 Does your family watch DVDs on TV?

Yes / No. We **always** / **never** watch DVDs.

5 Does your mum eat meat?

Yes / No. She **always** / **never** eats meat.

2 **Look at the calendar. Write always or never.**

Anna: What does he do in January?

Bill: He _____ celebrates New Year's Day.

Anna: Does he celebrate New Year's in February, too?

Bill: No. He _____ celebrates New Year's in February! That's silly.

January

	Mon	Tues	Wed	Thu	Fri	Sat	Sun
	1 New Year's Day	2	3	4	5	6	7
	8	9	10	11	12	13	14
	15	16	17	18	19	20	21
	22	23	24	25	26	27	28
	29	30	31				

Write these words in your own language.

Unit 1	SB Page
classroom	4
colouring	4
counting	4
cutting	4
gluing	4
listening	4
playing a game	4
using the computer	4
watching a DVD	4
writing	4
one hundred	10
equals	10
minus	10
plus	10
take turns	16
bath	17
both	17
crocodile	17
Maths	17
mouth	17
path	17
teeth	17
then	17
thin	17
with	17

My favourite word:

Unit 2	SB Page
climbing trees	20
doing gymnastics	20
flying kites	20
ice skating	20
playing tennis	20
playing volleyball	20
riding my bike	20
skateboarding	20
like	21
love	21
playground	21
running	21
swing	21
together	22
team	23
bones	26
kick	26
muscles	26
take care of	26
throw	26
each side	32
helmet	32
in front of	32
knee pads	32
safely	32
slide	32

	SB Page
seesaw	32
bang	33
bank	33
ink	33
king	33
ring	33
sink	33
wing	33

My favourite word:

Unit 3	SB Page
bathroom	36
bed	36
bedroom	36
chair	36
cooker	36
cupboard	36
dressing table	36
DVD player	36
fridge	36
kitchen	36
lamp	36
living room	36
sofa	36
table	36
TV	36
behind	37

Wordlist

glasses	37
in	37
keys	37
on	37
put on	37
aunt	38
cousin	38
uncle	38
quiet	39
between	40
next to	40
under	40
phone	41
new	42
old	42
wheel	42
dirty	48
dishes	48
tidy	48
toy box	48
washing machine	48
cook	49
cool	49
moon	49
zoo	49

My favourite word:

Unit 4	**SB Page**
bank	58

bookshop	58
bus stop	58
cinema	58
computer shop	58
petrol station	58
post office	58
restaurant	58
shopping centre	58
supermarket	58
town	58
train station	58
buy	59
eat	59
far	59
letter	59
map	59
near	59
send	59
first	60
hungry	60
wallet	61
film	62
boat	64
go to school by	64
train	64
cross the road	70
last	70
left	70

pedestrian crossing	70
right	70
second	70
wait	70
drive	71
nail	71
oak	71
rain	71
sail	71
soap	71
tail	71
wear	71

My favourite word:

Unit 5	**SB Page**
actor	74
artist	74
athlete	74
chef	74
dancer	74
doctor	74
dream job	74
pilot	74
singer	74
teacher	74
vet	74
writer	74
farmer	80
hairdresser	80

nurse	80	shadow	96	tomatoes	112
park ranger	84	sundial	96	vegetables	112
protect	85	tell time	96	yoghurt	112
Science	86	use	96	chips	113
Art	86	work	96	fruit	113
Music	86	early	102	ice cream	113
set goals	86	on time	102	share	113
study hard	86	quickly	102	pie	115
My favourite word:		ready	102	disease	118
		chin	103	fat	118

Unit 6	**SB Page**	chop	103	healthy	118
o'clock	90	rich	103	heart	118
do my homework	91	ship	103	salt	118
evening	91	witch	103	sugar	118
get dressed	91	My favourite word:		avocado	123
get up	91			kiwi	123
go out	91	**Unit 7**	**SB Page**	pineapple	123
go to bed	91	apples	112	watermelon	123
sleep	91	bananas	112	chocolate	123
start school	91	burger	112	popular	123
stay in bed	91	carrots	112	bee	125
watch	91	cheese	112	cried	125
come back	92	mangoes	112	flies	125
in the afternoon	92	meat	112	lie	125
boring	93	oranges	112	sheep	125
finish school	94	potatoes	112	tie	125
cup	96	sandwiches	112	My favourite word:	
hourglass	96	snack	112		
sand	96	strawberries	112		

Wordlist

Unit 8	SB Page
cheetah	128
elephant	128
giraffe	128
hippo	128
kangaroo	128
monkey	128
parrot	128
peacock	128
polar bear	128
snake	128
wild	128
zebra	128
chase	129
at night	132
cold	134
colourful	134
dark	134
deer	134
desert	134
fox	134
jungle	134
lizard	134
plants	134
ocean	134
raccoon	134
seal	134
whale	134

	SB Page
amazing	136
appreciate	140
beautiful	140
clever	140
strong	140
clown	141
owl	141
route	141
soup	141
toucan	141

My favourite word:
_____

Unit 9	SB Page
April	144
August	144
December	144
February	144
January	144
July	144
June	144
March	144
May	144
November	144
October	144
September	144
excited	145
month	145
winter	146

	SB Page
summer	148
autumn	150
spring	150
wish	150
good luck	154
midnight	154
ring	155
ant	157
bat	157
rat	157

My favourite word:
_____

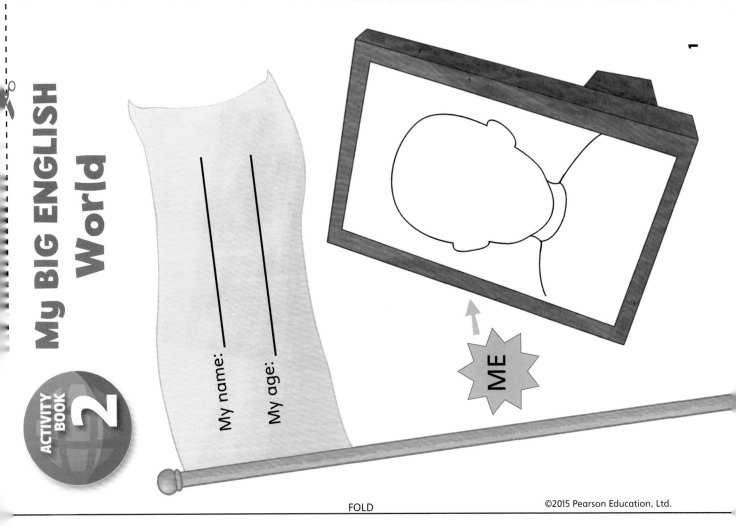

My BIG ENGLISH World

ACTIVITY BOOK 2

My name: _____

My age: _____

ME

FOLD

ENGLISH
AROUND ME

Paste or draw things with English words.

CINEMA TICKET

My Favourite Unit:

1 In My Classroom

2 Playground Fun

3 In My House

4 In My Town

My Favourite Words:

• supermarket
• hello • goodbye • computer
• skateboard • banana
bike • story • yoghurt

FOLD

5 My Dream Job

6 My Day

7 Food

8 Wild Animals

9 Fun All Year

My Favourite Project:

What do you like saying?

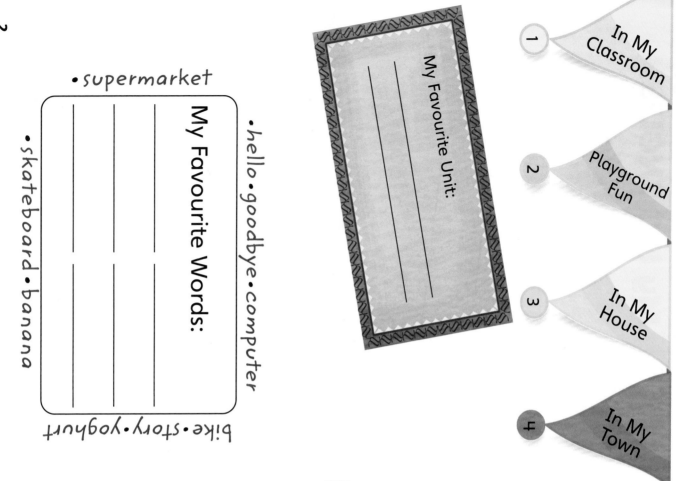